marimekko

Laird Borrelli-Persson

marimekko

The Art of Printmaking

Yale University Press

Laird Borrelli-Persson is Archive Editor at Vogue.com and author of seven books, including *Fashion Illustration Now* and *Fashion Illustration Next*, both published by Thames & Hudson.

ON THE COVER Suur Unikko (Large Poppy), Maija Isola, 1964 / Emma Isola, 2020.
ON P. 2 Babes in the wood: The Marimekko remix, photographed by Tony Vaccaro in 1965.
THIS PAGE Pieni Unikko II (Small Poppy II), Maija Isola, 1964 / Kristina Isola, 2009.
OVERLEAF Väriraita (Colour Stripe), Pentti Rinta, 1973, made into the Huomio skirt and Motti blouse, photographed by Osma Harvilahti at the Marimekko printing factory in Herttoniemi, Helsinki, 2020.

First published in North America by
Yale University Press
P.O. Box 209040
302 Temple Street
New Haven, CT 06520-9040
yalebooks.com/art

Published by arrangement with Thames & Hudson Ltd, London

Designed by Karin Fremer
Written by Laird Borrelli-Persson

Library of Congress Control Number: 2021931529

ISBN 978-0-300-25983-4

Printed and bound in Italy by Printer Trento SrL

10 9 8 7 6 5 4 3 2 1

Contents

1. Making Marimekko

At Marimekko, a dress has never been just a dress. It is a concept, a lifestyle, a manifesto – for freedom, peace, love and happiness. Armi Ratia, co-founder of this Finnish brand synonymous with joyful colours and bold prints, used these utopian ideals as a beacon as she worked towards building a brighter future from the rubble of post-war Helsinki. From day one, the company has placed importance on handcraft, creativity and collaborative effort, which gives its products an integrity that continues to stand out, even in this sometimes circus-like digital age.

It is tempting to believe that the charismatic Armi, who was known for her charm and force of character, simply willed Marimekko into being, but that is only partly true. Hindsight shows that the company answered a collective yearning for hope and beauty; but at the time, the story of the company's founding was one of luck and hard work, with Armi playing the role of the fairy-tale heroine who endures trials on her path to enlightenment.

'I think beauty is very necessary.'[4]

Armi Ratia

'Marimekko was born when I was born', Armi once declared.[1] The once-upon-a-time beginning of this tale is therefore specific rather than vague, as this entrepreneurial Finn, née Airaksinen, came into the world in the lake-rich territory of Karelia on 13 July 1912. In December 1917, soon after the fall of the Russian Empire, of which Finland had been a part, the country declared its independence; by January of the next year its citizens were fighting a civil war, which must have been upsetting for a five-year-old.

The daughter of a shopkeeper father and schoolteacher mother, Armi was, by her own account, 'difficult to understand as a child.'[2] Writing was her preferred means of creative expression, and when, in 1932, she moved to Helsinki to study textile design at the Central School for Applied Arts (now the Aalto University School of Arts, Design and Architecture), she supported herself by writing romance stories for magazines under a pseudonym. Maybe this made her extra susceptible to Cupid's arrow; in any case, on her graduation in 1935 Armi married Viljo Ratia, a career soldier she had met before moving to the city to study. 'I was too young', she would later say, 'but I was in love with his officer's uniform.'[3]

Viljo and his uniform would see service in the Winter and Second World Wars. A newly independent Finland, David to Russia's Goliath, fought for its existence in the Winter War. 'I believe for as long as I live I shall remember Finland's war of 1939–1940, its "Winter of Honour", when a whole people struggled for its freedoms beyond the limit of its abilities. Finland's

PREVIOUS SPREAD A Marimekko wonderland at Armi Ratia's summer house, Bökars, with Maija Isola fabrics hanging from the windows. From left: Holvi (Vault), 1964; Melooni (Melon), 1963; Seireeni (Siren), 1964; Silkkikuikka (Great-crested Grebe), 1961; and Kaivo (Well), 1964.
ABOVE Armi Ratia, Marimekko's big-hearted, occasionally imposing founder, 1974.

soldiers fighting in their white camouflage suits, the unbelievable cold, the unbelievable battle on the Karelian Isthmus, at Suomussalmi, at Petsamo', wrote Astrid Lindgren, best known as the 'mother' of Pippi Longstocking, in the war diaries she kept while working as a censor in Sweden's secret Postal Control Division.[5] At the conclusion of the conflict, in March 1940, Finland had to cede its south-eastern region, which included Karelia, to Russia. When Germany attacked the Soviet Union in 1941, Finland became a co-belligerent in what was known as the Continuation War, and after a peace treaty was made with Russia in 1944, Finland then fought with the Soviets against Germany. At the war's end Finland was free, but had to pay reparations to Russia, which also still claimed Karelia as its own, displacing thousands of Finns.

The result was that Armi and Viljo – who had been left homeless at the time of the Winter War – could never go home again. Armi would tell the story of her dispossession in various ways throughout her life. In one version, she leaves a burning Karelia 'with nothing but a raincoat and a gas mask that leaked.'[6] In another, unverified telling, Armi says, 'We burned our home when we left, rather than leave it to [the Russians]', adding, poignantly, 'all my golden coffee cups were

'Finland, which was depressing during and immediately after the war, needed some brightness.'[10]

Armi Ratia

broken.'[7] Those vessels might be stand-ins for what must have been her own shattered heart. By 1944 Armi had lost her home, two of her brothers and her brother-in-law, and was left, according to her own account, with only the dress on her back.

These traumatic events were formative ones. The result of losing everything was, Armi reflected, that 'everything always seems like a miracle to me.'[8] Not only did she come to find every day a gift, but to find joy and value in everyday objects. 'It's possible to find beauty in the simple things of home rather than in fancy possessions', she said.[9] Ideas about home

ABOVE Karelian refugees, Karelia, Finland, c. 1941.
OPPOSITE Helsinki-Helsingfors, Per-Olof 'PON' Nyström, 1951.
This pattern, which depicts many of the capital's landmarks, was reissued when Helsinki was named the 2012 World Design Capital.

and connection were of interest to her, and she was curious about people's relationship to their environment, be that architectural or natural.

In 1939, Armi had no time to mourn. She got a job at the Ministry of Defense (some American sources suggest she had been a spy).[11] Whatever she worked on while there, in 1942 this wordsmith took a job as a copywriter at Erva-Latvala Oy, an advertising agency in Helsinki. After seven years there, it was time, thought Armi, to retire to the mountains and write a novel. But fate would have it otherwise, and she unexpectedly started on a journey that was stranger than fiction.

Viljo was the unwitting protagonist in this plot twist. Having left the military, he invested in an old oilcloth factory, which soon went bankrupt. Viljo then bought the estate and founded his own company, Printex Oy. At his invitation, Armi joined Printex in 1949, and two years later Marimekko was incorporated. Thus, a phoenix rose from the ashes of war.

Post-war Helsinki was a grey place depleted by war, burdened by reparations and short on material resources. Yet the Finns, who had lived through unimaginable horrors, were free. For a new generation of bright-eyed idealists, the future was a blank slate ready to be filled with ideas for a better world. 'The war cleared our minds. Everything was taken away and we had to rethink. That was a very creative thing to happen', Armi said many years later. 'You see, when there are too many things in your life, you may go into a wilderness of possibilities. But crisis situations have good effects, they bring about new thinking.'[12]

According to company lore, Printex shifted from making coated cottons (oilcloth) to printed ones after Armi found printing materials in the factory. It is not too difficult to imagine the appeal of this kind of work to a one-time writer used to filling a white page with colourful, seductive, rhythmic words. She set about gathering a like-minded creative team and commissioning young artists to design new, bold patterns for the company. Among them was Maija Isola, then twenty-two, who would go on to create some of the most iconic Marimekko designs, including the Unikko (Poppy) print that now functions almost like a company logo. 'How much courage Armi had to have to start a company with that vision', says current employee Anna Hakkarainen, Head of North America, 'during the time when

'Artworks by artists who in the beginning were all young women, who were allowed full freedom to use their creativity on a blank fabric...'

Anna Hakkarainen

OPPOSITE Marimekko was a female-majority company from the start. Hand-screening continued until 1978; here, the Armi Ratia-designed Tiiliskivi (Brick), 1952, is being made.

Finland was just a poor country on the edge of the world and there were zero female executives around to show [an] example.'

In today's terms, Printex/Marimekko – the two companies coexisted for some time – might be described as a start-up operating on a shoestring budget. The team's learn-as-you-go process was unfettered by rules, expectations, or extensive experience, allowing for experimentation and innovation in print design and production. Free and expressive, their patterns were somewhat related to the pre-war work of the Austrian-born 'father of Swedish modernism' Josef Frank, but represented a new mode of expression that brought together graphic design with, as Armi told a journalist in 1972, 'a hint of Matisse and a suggestion of Slavic folk art.'[13]

Designer Vuokko Eskolin-Nurmesniemi, who joined Marimekko in 1953, has related that 'it was common in those days after the war to copy patterns.'[14] In contrast, Printex/Marimekko designs were sui generis and, moreover, they were treated like art: each pattern was named and the designer credited.

'I suppose I liked bold designs at that time because everyone else was doing small prints',[15] said Armi, who, with her team, not only broke with tradition, but literally broke free of borders: new colours were created when screens – intentionally or not – overlapped during the screenprinting process. Staying within the lines was not their style. Marimekko's archive is by now so vast that it includes patterns of all kinds, loud and quiet, big and small; yet the company is still primarily associated with the bright, expressive, airy aesthetic established in the early Printex days.

As attractive and cheering as they were, Printex fabrics turned out to be more ahead of the curve than consumers. 'No one bought the fabric...[they] didn't know what to do with it', Armi told *The Los Angeles Times* in 1968. 'So I tell them "go to hell." Excuse me, I learn my English from your Mr Hemingway. So I start to design dresses to use the fabric' (Armi, like Hemingway, pulled no punches).[16] These frocks were first introduced to the public on 20 May 1951 in a fashion show that Armi organized at the Kalastajatorppa Hotel, Helsinki.

OPPOSITE Amfora (Amphora), Maija Isola, 1949. Inspired by a museum exhibition, this early Isola pattern has a folksy, calligraphic touch. Its cursive quality is akin to the book covers designed by Bloomsbury Group artists for the Hogarth Press in the 1920s.
ABOVE Marimekko was registered days after Armi Ratia staged a fashion show of looks designed by Riitta Immonen using Printex fabrics on 20 May 1951.

It featured designs by Riitta Immonen, who worked Printex printed cottons into fairly typical waisted and fitted 1950s silhouettes. They were such a hit that Marimekko was registered as a company just days later.

Unsurprisingly, the new business was christened by its wordsmith founder. 'I had to come up with a name for the fashion collection quickly', Armi would later explain, 'so I thought of Mari, the name of the eternal woman, and Mekko which is a Finnish word for a simple dress.'[17] In 1956, Mari would meet her match when Eskolin-Nurmesniemi designed the striped Jokapoika – (Every Boy) – shirt, which has never gone out of production.

From the start, Marimekko has been a majority women company; it was the same more than sixty years later, in 2015.[18] After the war, Finland was rebuilt, and reimagined, by men and women working together. This equity was unusual enough to be remarked on by travel writer Frances Koltun, who, in 1962, described Finnish women as 'the most fulfilled of all women in the Western world, they feel free to work, to marry, to pursue careers, to have families, to care for husbands, all tasks good-humoredly handled in the same twenty-four-hour day, without ever expressing any of the psychological Sturm und Drang that seem to beset American women.'[19] Marimekko has always empowered women; the company is feminist in practice, but has never stridently pushed a feminist agenda. They have long produced unisex clothing, and Armi, who once sat for an interview wearing a pin that read 'I am a hippie', had a utopian outlook that was broadly inclusive.[20] 'I believe people should be very free to like what they want', she said. 'I'm not a priest for any culture or style.'[21]

> '**I'm selling a way of life. If you think Marimekko is fashion, you're lost. Marimekko is freedom from fashion – actually, a big laugh at establishmentarianism.**'[22]
>
> *Armi Ratia*

One of the ways in which Armi expressed her idealism was through a never-completed project to build Marikylä (Mari-village) where staff would reside and create, inspired, in part, by the concept of the 'global village' proposed by the scholar Marshall McLuhan. A prototype unit designed by the architect Aarno Ruusuvuori was built, but the idea never came to fruition. Still, Armi put many of the essentials into practice both in the factory and at her country house, Bökars, to which employees had regular invitations.

ABOVE The pre-fabricated 'Mari sauna', shown here in 1968, was designed
for Marimekko by the Finnish architect Aarno Ruusuvuori in 1966.

Eden cannot be recreated, but Marimekko employees had it made. In 1964, Beverley Wilson of *The Miami Herald* reported on some of their perks: 'At the Helsinki factory, employees take a regular coffee break in a horizontal position on cushions provided by the establishment, which also calls in hairdressers to work on them while they work, provides sauna baths, a breakfast table set for long hours, an open fire, a summer cottage, as well as guest beds.'[23] Marimekko might not have been a paradise, but it was a merry microcosm and a largely female enclave in which Armi played the role of mother, hostess, and madcap aunt.

'It's champagne today, worries tomorrow, chaos on Thursday. There are no prohibitions. Only independence and a respect for integrity.'[26]

Armi Ratia

The factory was a safe place that existed somewhat apart from the 'real' world, which Armi seemed to associate with (toxic) masculinity. 'What has my life among 333 women taught me?' she asked rhetorically in 1967. 'That I know few real men. It is wrong to bring up boys to be heroes who cannot weep. The world of men is so real.'[24] This might be a reference to Viljo, of whom Armi said after their divorce, 'My husband was in the army. I couldn't live with a warrior.'[25] Petri Juslin, a print design expert, offers an alternative reading, explaining that Armi's third brother was badly traumatized in the war and died young.

At Marimekko, freedom of thought was combined with freedom of movement in the silhouettes created by Eskolin-Nurmesniemi between 1953 and 1960. Much like the print designs of Isola and others played with white space, letting air into the design, these straightforward and unencumbered shapes, sacks and tents freed the body even as they housed the female form.

At the time Marimekko was founded, Finland was already famous for its architecture. In the pre-war period, Alvar Aalto saw his own house and the renowned Villa Mairea to completion. Designed by Yrjö Lindegren and Toivo Jäntti, and built in 1938, the Helsinki Olympic Stadium had its moment of glory in 1952 (the year after Marimekko was registered) when Finland hosted the games. 'Architects are so revered here, in fact, that Finland is probably the only country in the world where a newspaper could publish, as did a Finnish daily a few years ago, the headline: "Professor Saarinen Arrives from America" and add laconically, in small type, "Greta Garbo on Same Boat"', observed an American travel writer in 1962. 'Architecture is',

OPPOSITE The Mandara dress, designed by Liisa Suvanto, in a pattern created by Katsuji Wakisaka in 1971, pictured here at the Marimekko printing factory in 2020.

'My approach is something like the architect's.
He makes a house for people to live in.
I make a dress for a woman to live in.'[31]

Armi Ratia

she added, 'the over-riding passion, the greatest creative urge of the country, where, not having a tradition of heavily decorated buildings, simplicity and functionalism come naturally.'[27] Similarly, Marimekko dresses, designed around prints, needed no further adornment, and thus extended the Finnish architectural aesthetic into the sartorial realm – if not into fashion.

Armi declared Marimekko to be anti-fashion; clothing 'for the woman who wants to forget her dress...for such women as the many intellectuals we have in Finland, absorbed in writing books, in music, in art, in designing, who do not have to have such a fuss about what they put on'[28] (in other words, women like Armi and her colleagues). Marimekko, then, was for 'women who do', as opposed to women who are decorative; as such these garments had to work, to link form and function. It was closely aligned with the Bauhaus, and with Alvar Aalto's idea of organic modernism, which had both appeared before the Second World War.[29] The Bauhaus championed an interdisciplinary approach to design and aimed to bring artistry to industrial design, making it accessible to many. Marimekko's mission, to infuse the quotidian with joy, is clearly related to this way of thinking. Armi's belief in Bauhaus ideals is highlighted by a verbal snapshot of Armi, published in *The Boston Globe* in 1974: 'There behind the broad desk and cascading daisies in a glass bowl. Beneath the photo of [Bauhaus founder] Walter Gropius, she sits. The indomitable woman who created what must be the world's largest source of design excellence in cloth, personifies a lifestyle at once casual and total.'[30]

Armi's anti-fashion philosophy was likely also influenced, consciously or not, by Jantelagen, a moral and social code which exists in different forms across the Scandinavian region. It favours fitting in rather than standing out, conformity over individual expression, all in the interest, some would say, of equality. Timeless, trend-resistant designs work within this framework; fashion's snob appeal and status signalling does not. As the journalist Jane Holtz Kay put it, creating 'something agelessly fashionable' became for Armi 'the design way to defeat Obsolescence, Technology, Conspicuous

OPPOSITE Liisa Suvanto's Friisi dress, in the Knossos pattern by Katsuji Wakisaka, 1972.

Consumption, Class Snobbery and like heavies – the stick of good design beating the ills of the world.'[32]

Armi believed that women had more important things to consider than clothes – like nature. Many Marimekko prints, for example Kivet (Stones), designed by Maija Isola in 1956, are inspired by the outdoors. Time spent in nature was also considered in clothing design. 'We also do a great deal with play clothes. We have 40,000 lakes – think of all those beaches!', said Armi in 1959.[33] Minna Kemell-Kutvonen, Marimekko's Director of Home Design and Prints, suggests that the Finns' rural heritage has also led to the tradition of changing home textiles seasonally. Just as a Marimekko dress creates a shelter for the body, so its home products dress the home, often in a way that brings the outside in and reflects the extremes of a climate that veers from darkest winter to sunlit nights. In the company's vast print archive there is often a dialogue between opposites – decorative and minimalist, light and dark, rustic and urban, large and small.

> ## 'The shape, line and colour of everyday things are not so much appreciated as deeply felt by the Finns.'[35]
>
> *Dilys Rowe, The Observer*

In 1951, when Marimekko dresses took off locally, Finland had no fashion reputation to speak of outside the country. Armi would put the country on the fashion map at a time when the industry was excitedly discovering new centres of creativity. American *Vogue*, for example, debuted its first 'International Fashion Issue' in March 1953, writing: 'We couldn't have done such an issue before. Fashion only got its internationalization papers a short time ago....'[34]

To best contextualize Marimekko's impact on the industry, it is helpful to trace back to the Second World War. Paris had always been considered the capital of fashion; when the city was under Occupation, however, there was talk of moving couture, a French patrimony, to Berlin. Lucien Lelong, then president of the Chambre Syndicale de la Haute Couture, is credited with preventing the move. The course of post-war fashion was set in February 1947 when, during a bitterly cold winter, Christian Dior made his debut – and made history – with a collection that reasserted the survival, and primacy, of French fashion. The designer proposed an hourglass silhouette with sloping shoulders, a hand-span waist, and a full skirt made with incredible amounts of yardage. At a time when resources were short, it made an impact. Though dubbed the New Look, Dior had referenced *fin de siècle* silhouettes; the

OPPOSITE Armi Ratia, seen here in the 1960s, was a woman of gritty strength. In 1960, she visited New York and had this to say about women: 'the same with the rocks – stern, dreaming, harsh maybe, but often greatly individual and capable of winning.'[36]

Nature is the most constant source of inspiration at Marimekko:
OPPOSITE A suit in Maija Isola's Pioni (Peony), 1970, in a field of
sunflowers, Spring/Summer 2020.
ABOVE Marimekko-less in the woods in the 1960s, with a dress in
Annika Rimala's Pikkuruutu (Small Square), 1965, in the foreground.

collection was both nostalgic and romantic, supported by boning that moulded the body into curves – talk about architecture.

From that point on, Dior would introduce a new silhouette every season, but it was the fit-and-flare idea that became the predominant post-war look. Dior died in 1957, the same year that Cristóbal Balenciaga introduced the unfitted sack dress, an evolution of his tunic line that marked a sea-change in fashion. This 'loose and enveloping creation', wrote curator Miren Arzalluz, 'opened up a new and unprecedented space between body and garment, as well as a novel way for women to feel and move within the dress.… In this design', she continues, 'the woman's body became an abstract being that moved freely inside the unfamiliar space it now inhabited.'[37] Space in 1950s haute couture was usually equated to volume, as well as to taking up space in terms of social standing and clout. That is not the case at Marimekko, where space is equated with freedom. This was in keeping with a larger tendency in Finnish design, as observed by Dilys Rowe in 1962: 'perhaps the secret of the gifted restraint of Finnish design', she wrote, 'is that the Finns, from the habit of visualizing space, care as much for the surrounding void as for the shape itself.'[38]

Marimekko's 'straight-hanging' dresses were, said Armi, 'born out of my childhood apron and [the] eternal cleaning shirt of my later youth.'[39] As such, they were connected to local traditions and lifestyle. In contrast, Balenciaga's sack, though it appeared later, was a logical evolution of his development of silhouettes. It was fashion. Though Armi claimed not to care about *la mode*, it seems she 'doth protest too much', as she was keen that Marimekko innovations were credited. 'So some astonished European fashion magazines have proclaimed us "ahead of our time." Who's ahead of what?' she once queried. 'Who created the first op art dress, the Courrèges line, ankle-length hostess dresses? Our collection last summer contained an op coat, black and white, trapeze cut. It was a hit. I made it thirteen years ago', she asserted in 1967, 'so did we beat Paris? Another hit was a very short

ABOVE Summer love: Maija Isola's 1964 Unikko (Poppy) and 1969 Mansikkavuoret (Strawberry Hills) translated into sartorial treats for Spring/Summer 2021.
OPPOSITE Vuokko Eskolin-Nurmesniemi designed the print, Nadja, in 1959 and the Iloinen takki (Happy Coat) in 1960. It has been suggested that she created the small pockets as places to put small love tokens from her husband.[40]

'Ever hear of a Marimekko? In certain sophisticated fashion circles, it's part of the fashion language. The word and the thing come from Finland, of all places, and it means a style of little-nothing dress in colours and fabrics created by a workshop of the same name.'[44]

Florence de Santis, The Shreveport Times

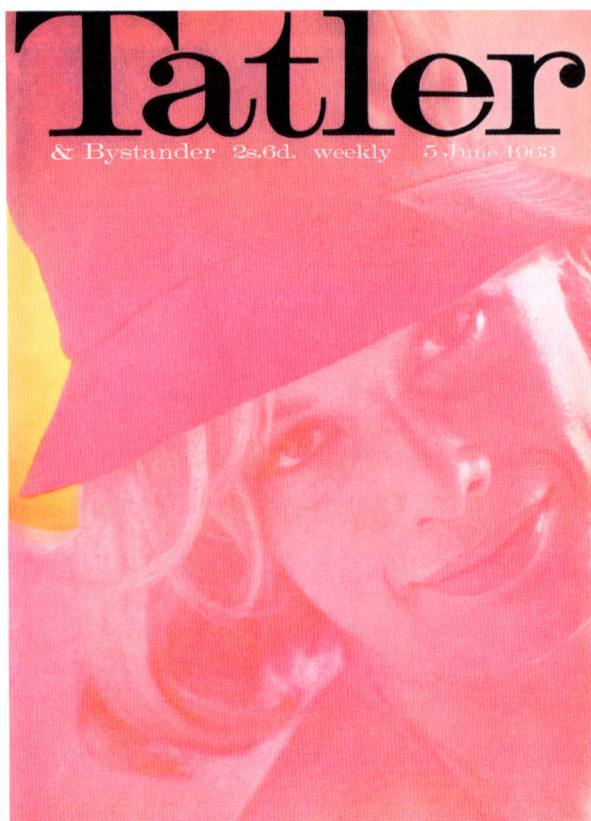

black and white dress. Féraud copy? No...it was only one of our children's dresses that had been around for ten years.'[41]

It was in the 1960s that the Marimekko aesthetic intersected most frequently with capital-F fashion; conceptually, though, they had little in common. Armi approached clothes as an extension of a philosophy of life that was connected to nature and the home; designer fashion, which is more closely tethered to passing trends, is always changing. If designer labels communicated wealth and social status, Marimekko signalled an alliance with a liberal, egalitarian point of view. 'Marimekko', noted the *San Francisco Examiner*, 'protested against the little black dress with pearls and a world of crystal chandeliers.'[42]

Part of the enduring appeal of Marimekko is that it manages at once to retain its quintessential Finnishness and have universal appeal. In her flippant, offhand way, Armi once attributed the company's success to 'the clairvoyance of Finnish witches and to the fact that people are the same everywhere.'[43] Outside Scandinavia, however, part of the brand's appeal is its Nordic otherness. In playing up the design aspect of the company, Marimekko aligned itself with the country's architects and product designers, not to mention what would become known as the mid-century aesthetic.

ABOVE A Marimekko hat on the cover of *Tatler*, June 1963.
OPPOSITE Unikko reaches new heights in the form of a parasol, photographed by Tony Vaccaro in 1965.

'[Marimekkos] have the quality of thinking.'[45]

Armi Ratia

ABOVE Marimekko designs on display in Design Research's Orange County store, 1960s.
OPPOSITE In 1960, Jacqueline Kennedy bought nine Marimekko dresses at the Design Research 'summer store' store in Hyannis, Massachusetts, and wore them while summering at the Kennedy Compound in Hyannis Port. She was pictured in one of them on the December 1960 cover of *Sports Illustrated*.

After an exhibition of prints at the World's Fair in Brussels in 1958,[46] Armi received an invitation from the architect and Harvard professor Benjamin Thompson to be a part of an exhibition in his Design Research store in Cambridge, Massachusetts, which has since been credited with bringing 'modern living to American homes'.[47] Armi brought one hundred dresses along with the signature prints. They were a runaway success. 'Design Research...has sold over a hundred of these dresses since the summer, and this is not even a ready-to-wear shop, their specialties are contemporary furniture and furnishings from all over the world', noted *The Boston Globe* in 1959. 'The Marimekko line are the only dresses carried. And they are tucked away in a corner upstairs. You actually need to hunt for them!'[48] College students happily put in the effort, following which, reported fashion critic Eugenia Sheppard, 'hundreds of Radcliffe girls took it home to their mothers, and so the fad began.'[49]

The 'fad' was accelerated when Jacqueline Kennedy bought a number of Marimekkos at Design Research, and a photograph of her wearing one of them appeared on the cover of *Sports Illustrated* in 1960. An Associated Press journalist observed that Kennedy's choice of Marimekko was a logical extension of her 'well-known interest in chic, Avant Garde clothes.'[50]

By 1962, Sheppard reported that 'instead of buying dress-dresses, women have been flocking to buy Marimekkos, Lillys and Mumus.'[51] (Lilly is the name for printed dresses and resort-wear separates designed in Palm Beach by Lilly Pulitzer; the muumuu is a loose-fitting Hawaiian dress.) In 1963, 70,000 Marimekkos were reportedly made, and Sheppard, still on the case, declared: 'What Lilly Pulitzer has done for socialites, a charming, fresh-faced Finnish woman, Armi Ratia, has done for intellectuals – given them a uniform.' Both designers, she continued, 'reduce fashion to a common denominator of simplicity.... The Lilly may be fashion, but the Marimekko is design.'[52] (Emilio Pucci was also creating print-centric work at this time.) *Vogue*'s Diana Vreeland welcomed the Youthquake in 1965, enthusing: 'Youth, warm and gay as a kitten yet self-sufficient as James Bond, is surprising countries east and west with a sense of assurance

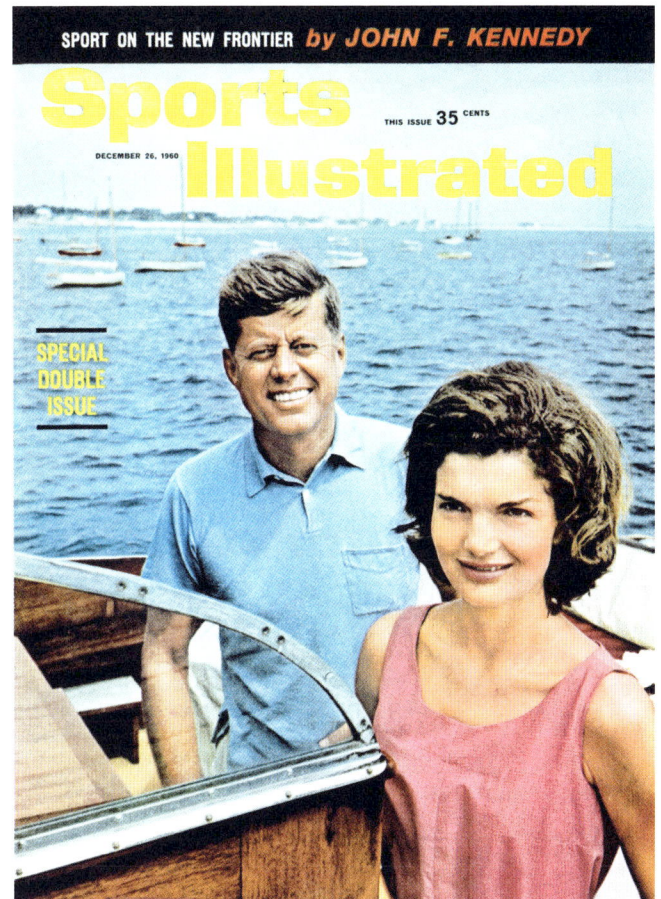

serene beyond all years.... The year's in its youth, the youth in its year. Under twenty-four and over 90,000,000 strong in the U.S. alone. More dreamers. More doers. Here. Now.'[53] Mary Quant was speaking to this new generation in their own language, and so was Marimekko. Armi was fifty-three in 1965; seven years later a journalist noted that the Finn was inspired by 'music, nature and the young way of life.'[54]

Marimekko was responsive to the big changes happening at the time: in 1968, Annika Rimala created an assortment of unisex pieces that could be worn with jeans, which included pieces in her Tasaraita (Even Stripe) pattern, introducing knits to the clothing line. Marimekko employee Marjaana Alanko 'grew up surrounded by Marimekko prints', and says, 'My favourite was a long Tasaraita night dress that I got from my godparents for my ninth birthday. I wore it day and night!' Marimekko's separation from the fashion system seemed to support independent, out-of-the-box thinking. 'It's gauche to ask where you're supposed to wear a Marimekko, long or short', noted a reporter in 1964. 'This is decided by the notably individualistic wearer of the dress, not the occasion. You either understand this way of dressing or you never will.'[55]

'In the traditional danger in which we live in Finland, and our comparatively hard life, unnecessary things fall away. We absolutely want the joy of life; without this we could not survive.'[58]

Armi Ratia

When *The Boston Globe* wrote in 1972 that 'flower power is Armi's line', the journalist was referring to the company's floral prints, not the hippie ethos, but both meanings apply.[56] In 1964, Maija Isola created Unikko, the poppy pattern that broke with the abstract look the company was known for and, defying Armi's ban on florals (see p. 55), opened a new chapter in the art of printmaking.

Printex designs were not conceived specifically for fashion design – in fact many dress patterns were built around the prints. Rather, they responded to a yearning for colour and happiness, and a need to celebrate life. Large, abstract designs broke from existing norms, but the past was not jettisoned. Isola's 1966 Juhannus (Midsummer) design, for example, incorporates folk elements. Preservation of the past in new contexts was a concept that Armi implemented in her own life when she had her grandparents' home dismantled, transported, and rebuilt at her summer place, Bökars.[57]

OPPOSITE A swatch card showing colour-ways of Juhannus (Midsummer), Maija Isola, 1966.

52

54

56

58

60

62

63

65 *52*

© MARIMEKKO OYJ SUOMI-FINLAND MAIJA ISOLA 1954 / E.I 2020: "MUSTA TAMMA"   100% CO   W 太 図 晶 ® 쎂   100% CO   W

ABOVE Musta Tamma (Black Mare), Maija Isola, 1954.
OPPOSITE Kaunis Kauris (Beautiful Deer), Teresa Moorhouse, 2011.

Armi was perhaps most at home in her factory, which she described as a 'big informal company run like a family – on impulse, accident and fancy!'[59] She quickly progressed from being a Jack – or Jill – of all trades to the creative direction, and though she was largely hands-off, the company's vast array of products carries her signature. When she did put pen to paper, she didn't use her name as a sign-off, as she relates an amusing tale recounted to *The Chicago Tribune*: 'I was having trouble with my cost advisors. They found ways to cut down on my expenses. They made me take out the word "love" from my cables. I always sign my letters and cables: "Love Marimekko". When Roger Horchow [an American retailer] wrote asking me where his deliveries were, I sent him a cable "Why are you so damn late sending me your orders?" But I signed it: "Love, M." That is our way. Now I put it back again, the love, because that is what we are.'[60]

Love, as is well known, does not pay the bills, and several times in its seventy-year history Marimekko was on the brink of financial disaster. In the 1970s, fashion moved towards closer-to-the-body looks, like Diane von Furstenberg's easy-on, easy-off wrap dresses. Marimekko's focus during the 'Me Decade' was largely on licensing, as well as internal and technological growth. All prints had been hand-screened until 1973, when the opening of a new printing facility allowed for mechanical production. Armi died in 1979, the year that all printing was moved to the new location. Sadly, she was unable to see the complete integration of all staff – printers, designers and executives – at Herttoniemi, which remains the company headquarters.

In 1985, Armi's heirs sold the company to Amer-yhtymä, a Finnish conglomerate, but it wasn't a good match. Kirsti Paakkanen bought the company in 1991 and reinvigorated it from the inside out, hiring new designers and, in 1992, inaugurating a public fashion show in Helsinki's

OPPOSITE Maija Isola's somewhat trippy Mansikkavuoret (Strawberry Hills) pattern was designed in 1969, the same year as Woodstock. It appears here as a tablecloth and on Oiva (Excellent) ceramics, in good company with a dress in the Mansikka (Strawberry) print created by Isola two years earlier, in 1967.
ABOVE Oiva tableware, designed by Sami Ruotsalainen, featuring the Ruudut (Squares) pattern, 2019.
OVERLEAF Marimekko's fashion show in Helsinki's Esplanade Park has become a summertime tradition for the brand – shown here in 2019.

'I really don't sell clothes. I sell a way of living. They are designs, not fashions…. I sell an idea rather than dresses.'[63]

Armi Ratia

Esplanade Park, which remains an ongoing summertime tradition. Since Mika Ihamuotila became the majority owner in 2007, his focus has been on expansion, both in terms of product offerings and global reach. In 2015, Ihamuotila was joined in these efforts by longtime Marimekko employee Tiina Alahuhta-Kasko, as the company's President and CEO.

Marimekko has become an important part of Finland's visual identity; the country's National Biography notes that the company 'and its products are a part of the Finns' conception of what it is to be a modern Finn.'[61] Present-day employees pay testament to that: 'Growing up in Finland, Marimekko had always been embedded in my life in bits and pieces here and there: a metal tray in the kitchen, curtains at my aunt's house, my grandmother's dress in the attic', says Anna Hakkarainen. 'My first memory of Marimekko was as a child', relates Annika Friman, 'where I went to a cabin in the Finnish woods. Inside the cabin, it was decorated with Unikko pillowcases on the sofa and they also had the towels in the bathroom. After a long day of being outside it was so cosy to sit in the sofa with the pillows and drink hot chocolate.' Ines Lakanen calls Marimekko 'a loyal friend at our household, bringing joy to the day.'

Marimekko is modern at the same time that it is deeply rooted in the culture of a relatively new country. Its products speak to Finland's democratic ideals in ways that have global as well as local appeal. Armi, noted *The Guardian,* 'has cleverly built up what has become virtually a Marimekko cult, in Scandinavia a way of life. Marimekko people spend their leisure in Marimekko-curtained log houses with saunas by lakesides wearing Marimekko dresses, eating off Marimekko table cloths. They live informally, nonchalantly; they are essentially modern and madly Marimekko.'[62]

OPPOSITE A matching shirt and backdrop in Fujiwo Ishimoto's Talkoot (Work Party), 1978, for pre-Spring 2020.
ABOVE Maija Isola's 1950 Appelsiini (Orange) print, used for the Sitruuna (Lemon) wrap skirt, Varjossa (Shade) hat and Sitrus (Citrus) wrap top. The pattern is said to have been inspired by a trip to Barcelona.

The company also internalized Finland's feminist ideals. 'I sell a new woman', said Armi, who was the very model of one.[64] Her influence continues to be felt in 2020. Marimekko employee Julia Kronlund recalls her mother looking 'particularly proud and strong' wearing her Marimekko dress, 'and one time she explained to me...the woman behind the dress and the brand was one of her role models. A woman who always stood up for her beliefs, always went her own way, no matter what others were saying or doing. And had an ambition to lift other women. All those values that my mother so strongly believed in. And today I have it as my job to make sure her vision is not forgotten.'

Marimekko's brand of utopianism remains relevant. The COVID-19 pandemic found many people at home, reconnecting with their roots and finding solace in quotidian pleasures like a sunny day, tea sipped from a favorite mug. Marimekko consistently delivers a message of hope. The company was founded, wrote a journalist in 1972, 'to be a fresh, new way of looking at things. When the Second World War ended, Mrs Ratia and her husband were left with nothing. The war experience changed her. Losing all her possessions caused Mrs Ratia to start thinking more freely, no longer constrained by the traditions of the past. Taking for granted ceased. "I gave a damn", she says.'[65]

OPPOSITE Among the rotary printing screens in Marimekko's factory, Herttoniemi. Left, the Nelikulmio (Rectangle) dress, 2021, in Antti Kekki's Kiila (Wedge) print, 2019, and right, the classic Jokapoika (Every Boy) shirt, the Kantakulma (Base Angle) trenchcoat, 2021, in Maija Isola's Seireeni (Siren) print, 1964, and a bright yellow Milli Matkuri (Milli-Traveller) bag.

2. The Art of Printmaking

Armi Ratia's own sense of wonder and utopianism has been woven into the fabric of Marimekko since the very start. 'It is wonderful to look at life through a child's eyes', she once said. 'This is not something new...but it is something that today I think there is more need for. Purity, simplicity, truth – unconfused by the complexity of the external world.'[1]

Considering the losses that she experienced as Finland fought to maintain its independence during the Second World War, the Marimekko founder's resilience and optimism is quite extraordinary. As she saw it, the path towards a better world was through creative expression and the integration of art into daily life. Armi chose print design as her medium, and created a playground for artists, a world apart where fantasies could come alive through colour and line.

From its earliest days as Printex, printmaking has remained so central to Marimekko that the company's present-day headquarters are built around the Marimekko printing factory, located in Herttoniemi, East Helsinki. All Marimekko prints were hand-screened until 1973, when the Herttoniemi factory first opened and a flatbed screen-printing machine was put into use. By 1979, all printing was mechanical – though many processes, from adding ink to the screens (see pp. 64–65) to checking lengths of printed cloth, still rely on expert hands and eyes. At Marimekko, machines work in concert with artisans, just as art meets engineering in the translation of original artworks to a reproducible print design.

Many Marimekko patterns have a direct and expressive – some would say childlike – quality, born of free expression. Armi wanted to push boundaries, not stay within the lines; as a result, 'naive' is an adjective frequently used to describe Marimekko prints, though that rather misses the point. 'It is not so simple to be simple in clothes, or in anything', Armi noted. 'It takes training to learn what to accept as a necessity when it looks like a luxury – and vice versa.'[2]

Primary colours seem particularly well-suited to bring to life the many so-called 'naive' prints in Marimekko's catalogue, often to electrifying effect. 'For the first time, garden colors were liberated – blues with greens, purple with pinks, pure orange with clarion scarlet',[3] enthused one American journalist in the 1970s, the decade of exuberant prints such as Kukkatori (Flower Market, Maija Isola, 1970; p. 156), Karuselli (Carousel, Katsuji Wakisaka, 1973; p. 115) and Kuuma (Hot, Fujiwo Ishimoto, 1978; p. 150).

Armi declared, 'I know all about colours because I feel them in everything...colours and people interact, affecting changes in one another. It is the deepest mystery.'[4] In 1949, the first year of her tenure at Printex, she

PREVIOUS SPREAD Fabric being hand-screened by printers at work in their own Marimekko dresses, photographed by Tony Vaccaro in 1965.
OPPOSITE Lengths of Maija Isola's Silkkikuikka (Great-crested Grebe) and Lokki (Seagull) patterns from 1961 hanging in Isola's summer studio in Suomenlinna fortress, Helsinki.

had proposed colour as an antidote to Helsinki's bleak post-war 'uniform' of grey, and administered it like a visual shot of vitamin D. At Marimekko today, brilliant hues remain a way to express joy as well as to create an atmosphere. Winters in Finland are awfully long, dark and very cold, and Marimekko's many-hued textiles and homewares bring cheer, light and a sense of warmth to interiors; in spring and summer, they mirror the abundance of nature in full bloom.

There are prints of every kind in Marimekko's archive. Whatever the style or era of the design, expressive or controlled (Armi herself designed some strict geometric grids; see Tiiliskivi, 1952, pp. 178–79, and Faruk, 1952, p. 183), there is a sort of 'freehand' energy to Marimekko patterns that can be linked to the individualistic approach that has always been encouraged in its designers. 'Mrs Ratia believes her most important contribution to Finnish design has been her willingness to leave her designers alone', a stringer for *The New York Times* wrote in a profile of 'Finland's Spirited Designer' in 1979. 'That kind of freedom, plus the isolation that has forced Finnish artists to create, rather than copy, she suggests, has built this country's reputation for inventive design.'[5] With Marimekko's print specialists on hand, artists needn't worry about neatly 'staying within the lines'; in fact, they are urged to experiment and explore. In collaboration with the brand's artwork studio, patterns have been conjured from such materials as cut paper (Kivet, Maija Isola, 1956; pp. 86–87), twigs (Lumimarja, Erja Hirvi, 2004; pp. 100–3) and pieces of contact paper (Teippi, Teija Puranen, 2013; pp. 106–7), and this spirit of innovation is now further enabled by cutting-edge technologies.

Marimekko's present-day focus on global expansion hinges on technology not only in design, but also for its operations and logistics. Data, says Tiina Alahuhta-Kasko, the company's President and CEO, can help to tailor products and experiences to hyperlocal markets in ways that speak respectfully to different cultures and climates. In collaboration with various educational institutions and private companies, Marimekko is also investigating how technological innovations can advance its ongoing efforts to become more sustainable.

Armi was thinking sustainably long before the subject became topical. Marimekko products have always been created to last, materially and aesthetically, beginning with the fabrics themselves. There's plenty of

> ## 'I am humble with designers. I tell them, find yourself, then it works.'[6]
>
> *Armi Ratia*

OPPOSITE Maija Isola's 1968 Taifuuni (Typhoon) waiting to be washed after printing. The company acquired its first automated printing machine in 1973; hand and machine work continued side-by-side until 1978.

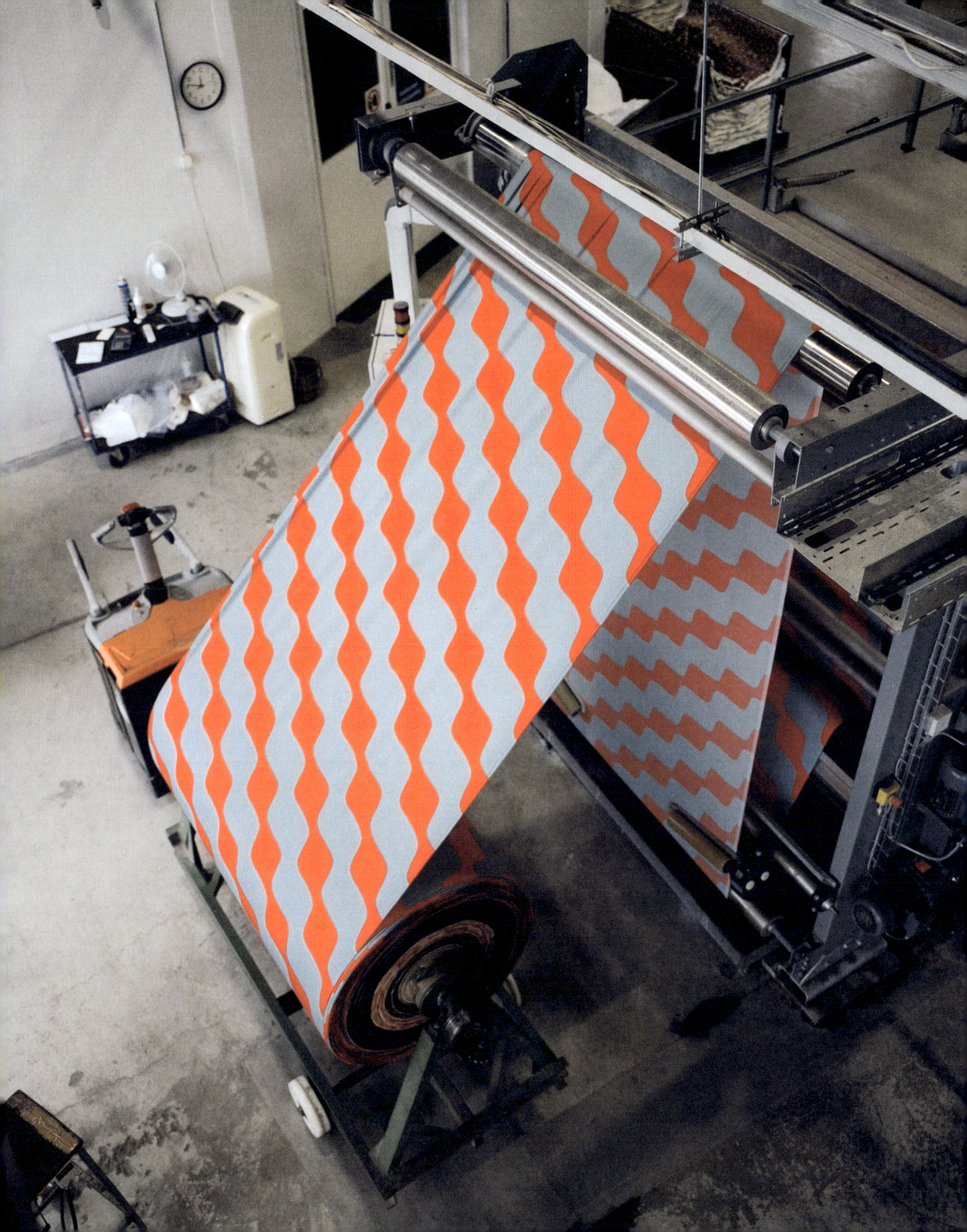

evidence that they do. 'I remember my mum explaining how Tasaraita shirts last forever. They do,' says Marjaana Alanko, Digital Marketing Manager, Australia. Her colleague, Lea Aarinen-Koski, Marimekko's Head of Licensing and Wholesale, Finland, and the sixth of six daughters in her family to wear a Tasaraita shirt, concurs.

'We took the lowest class of fabric, cotton, and we have made it fashionable', Armi once said.[7] Today, the company is experimenting with using a variety of more earth-friendly materials throughout its manufacturing processes, including textiles made of wood fibres. Marimekko is also thinking responsibly, and locally, by expanding its use of recycled raw materials and continuing to do a significant part of its printing at its factory and headquarters in Herttoniemi.

OPPOSITE Cold, dark Finnish winters heighten the longing for sun and the ripe abundance of summer. Yards of Maija Louekari's Pala Taivasta (Patch of Sky), 2019, have a transportative, tropical vibe.

UNIKKO

'Flower power is Armi's line', declared *The Boston Globe* in 1972 – but it wasn't always that way.[8] Despite the Finn's free-spirited style, blooms were initially banned from Marimekko print designers' work. Armi was on record as saying something along the lines of 'only nature could create something as beautiful as flowers.'[9] (It is also possible that the ban was instated with old-fashioned floral fabrics, so expressive of outdated ideas of decorative femininity, in mind.) When Maija Isola designed Unikko in 1964, it was an act of rebellion against Armi's edict.

But nothing in the print's generous curvilinear forms signals protest. Instead, the design that has come to serve as a de facto logo for Marimekko is irresistibly seductive and joyous. Poppies are a common sight in Scandinavia, where they are often seen punctuating the borders of golden fields of wheat and barley. It is said that they also grew in Isola's own yard. While some poppies are a source of opium, there is nothing at all sleepy about Unikko, with its bold rounds of colour punctuated with black centres and stems that seem to pop out of the background of the four-screen pattern.

Après Unikko, le déluge – or more accurately, *le jardin*. Armi gradually came around to liking flowers in real life and in print design. Given her expansive personality, it's no surprise that she favoured the wild ones. There have been florals in nearly every Marimekko collection since 1964.

OPPOSITE Unikko (Poppy), Maija Isola, 1964. This is one of its three original colour-ways.
ABOVE Unikko segues easily from wall to wardrobe, in a pleated Lepatus (Flutter) top and Viserrys (Twitter) skirt.

Unikko has been constantly in production since it was first introduced
in 1964. One of the wonders of this design is how easily it is refreshed
by a change of scale, colour or material.
OPPOSITE Unikko (Poppy), Maija Isola, 1964.
ABOVE Pieni Unikko II (Small Poppy II), Maija Isola, 1964 / Kristina
Isola, 2009.

Unikko was made in protest against Armi Ratia, who had forbidden the design of floral patterns.

Maija Isola, a painter and textile designer, was hired by Armi Ratia and had a nearly forty-year association with Marimekko. By the time she retired in 1987, Isola had created about 500 prints for the company, including signature patterns like Kivet (Stones) and Unikko (Poppy), which broke new ground in terms of textile design.
ABOVE From left: Isola painting in her studio; Unikko colour samples; hand-screening in the early years.
OPPOSITE Juhla Unikko (Celebration Poppy) rendered in a long-sleeved shift dress for the pre-Spring 2021 season.

ABOVE AND OPPOSITE Four screens are required to make Unikko in its classic colour-way. The dark navy stems are printed first, followed by the large red petals, the smaller pink ones, and finally, the orange centres, which overlap with the petal colour, adding depth to the print.

LEFT Marimekko yardage is proudly printed at the company's vast factory in Herttoniemi, Eastern Helsinki, where humble cotton is elevated with sophisticated, modern designs. Here, yardage is being fed into a rotary screen-printing machine. Wrinkles are removed before the fabric is printed with the four colours needed for Unikko. Note the printing machine's four screen rollers, at the top left of the image. All prints are checked by eye after printing.

RIGHT Lokki (Seagull) in production on a flat-bed printing machine. The ink is skillfully thrown across the screen, parts of which are blocked off. The ink is then forced through the porous parts of the screen to form the pattern. OVERLEAF Unikko being printed in black and white. All Marimekko prints measure 144 cm (about 54 in.) in width, with white margins on which the name of the print, designer and date are listed.

Unikko is no ordinary flower. Maija Isola's
design has a chameleon-like ability to change
and adapt to new visions and eras.
ABOVE Suur Unikko (Large Poppy), Maija Isola,
1964 / Emma Isola, 2020.
RIGHT 50th Anniversary Unikko, Maija Isola,
1964 / Kristina Isola, 2013.
OPPOSITE Ruutu-Unikko (Checked Poppy),
Maija Isola, 1964 / Emma Isola, 2014.

ABOVE AND OPPOSITE Three generations of Isolas have designed for Marimekko: Maija, her daughter Kristina and Kristina's daughter, Emma. Emma Isola's literally remixed version of her grandmother's most famous design was released in 2021, the company's seventieth year. With the Marimekko team, she came upon her marbleized technique while experimenting with a hand screen. Filled with a swirl of blues, it almost feels like the blooms are transparent and one is looking through poppy-shaped windows in the fabric.

ABOVE AND OPPOSITE Unikko's versatility extends far beyond the printing factory. The pattern has been applied to all sorts of products, from bedding to fashion and home furnishings.

COLOUR THINKING

Like light, colour is known to have therapeutic properties. The Finnish architect Alvar Aalto took this into consideration when designing the Paimio Sanatorium in the early 1930s, as would the printmakers at Marimekko from the 1950s onwards.[10]

Colour is a science and an art at Marimekko. 'Marimekko prints are always new because I have a colourist who never says no to a colour. You won't find that anywhere else', Armi once boasted.[11] It's a claim that holds true today. The company's ever-expanding colour library contains an almost unimaginable number of colours – about six thousand in 2020 – and that doesn't take into account the shades that are created through overlaps in the printing process.

Though print designers have access to the entire range of the spectrum, Marimekko is famous for the artful use print and textile designers have made of saturated brights – 'Matisse colours', as Armi once described them.[12] They're present in the pure, overlapping blocks of Vuokko Eskolin-Nurmesniemi's Hennika (1953, right and opposite), across the cars and trucks parked on Katsuji Wakisaka's Bo Boo design of 1975, and in a multitude of other designs. (This writer's childhood bedroom was outfitted with the four-colour Seven Flowers motif.)

Adding to the effectiveness of many Marimekko prints is the way that colour is liberated by the use of white space, and accentuated or framed with touches of black. Intensifying these contrasts was Armi's insistence on the clarity of colour, 'It used to be popular to sprinkle black into colors to dull them', she said in a 1972 interview. 'I said take out all the black, clean up the reds and the greens. Colours must be clean and true; blue from the seas, red from the tulips.'[13]

ABOVE AND OPPOSITE Free rein has been given to imagination and experimentation since Marimekko's early days, as is evidenced by swatch cards in the archive that record the many colour-ways of the different prints. The ones above are for the Hennika stripe, designed by Vuokko Eskolin-Nurmesniemi in 1953 and shown in full opposite, which creates its darker stripes through overlapping colours.
OVERLEAF Indus, Vuokko Eskolin-Nurmesniemi, 1953, and Husaari (Hussar), Maija Isola, 1966. In both patterns the stripes' grid is disrupted by the overlapping colours and unexpected spacing and quality of line.
PP. 78–79 Eskolin-Nurmesniemi's delicate black and white Suolampi (Marsh Pond) and Nadja, both 1959.

PREVIOUS SPREAD Four colour-ways
of Maija Isola's Mansikkavuoret
(Strawberry Hills), which was designed
in 1969, two years after the Beatles' hit
song 'Strawberry Fields Forever'.
RIGHT AND OPPOSITE Fujiwo Ishimoto's
Ostjakki (Khanty) and Jäkälä (Lichen),
both 1983. Both designs were inspired
by a book depicting the life of the
Finno-Ugrian peoples, as well as by
textiles patterned using traditional ikat
dyeing techniques.
OVERLEAF Seven colour-ways of Katsuji
Wakisaka's Kumiseva (Echoing), 1971,
showing how the print has changed
to reflect the times. Note the bright
oranges, pinks and purples of the
1970s, and the more muted palette of
the 2010s.

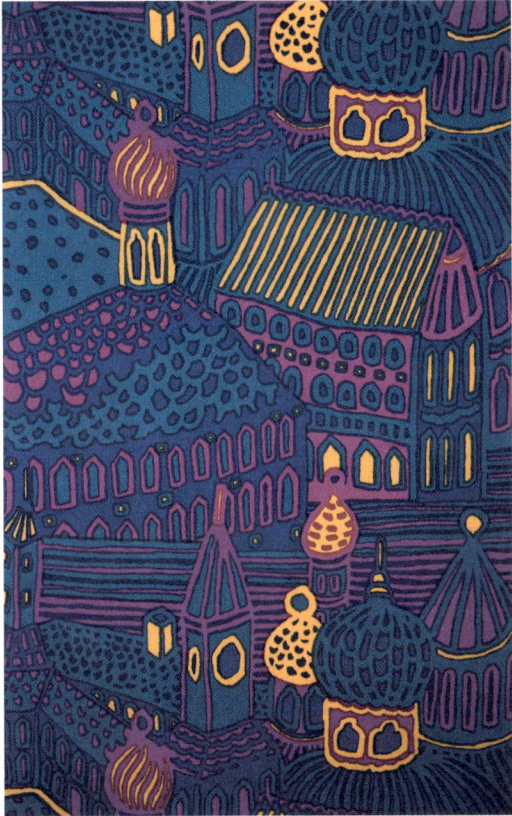

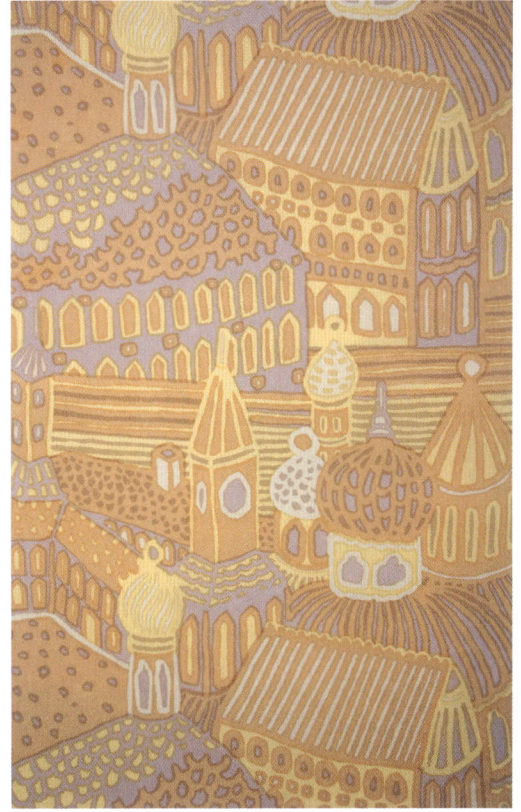

PERFECT
IMPERFECTIONS

It is always possible to find a human touch, a trace of the hand, in a Marimekko print. That perfect imperfection is the company signature. Every length of cloth is 'framed' by selvedge edges on which the title of the print, its designer and the year in which it was designed is indicated, much as a work of fine art might be credited.

In the years of hand screen-printing, allowances had to be made for tiny imperfections in 'registration' – the layering of colours, screen by screen, to create a pattern. A petal's colour bleeds outside its black outline; skinny, varying stripes overlap and blend a little. Marimekko's printing technicians learned not only to accommodate but to celebrate these elements of the process. Many of the company's breakthroughs were the result of enthusiastic experimentation and happy accidents, a number of which occurred in the printing process, where the raw fabric peeked through, or a frame left a mark on the heavy cotton.

In 2020, when technology enables near-perfection, Petri Juslin, a print design expert, has observed designers combining the use of digital tools with the more homely hand techniques of yore. Examples of this include Siirtolapuutarha (City Garden, p. 124) and Kasvio (Flora, p. 153), among others.

One of the reasons a Marimekko print can deliver everyday joy, whatever the materials or the methods used in its making, is because it continues to preserve this relatable, perfectly imperfect feel.

ABOVE Maija Isola designed Kivet (Stones), 1956, using paper cut-outs. Their imperfect edges, much like the fabric circles on this sample, were translated into the two-screen print, where they are further highlighted by the overlap between the circles and their background.
OPPOSITE Isot Kivet (Big Stones), Maija Isola, 1959.

ABOVE, RIGHT AND OPPOSITE Maalaisruusu (Country Rose) was a part of the same batch of floral patterns as Unikko (Poppy, pp. 54–71), rebelliously designed by Maija Isola in 1964. The flowers look identical at first glance, but upon looking closely their differences begin to reveal themselves.

OPPOSITE AND RIGHT Maija Isola hand-painted her design for Silkkikuikka (Great-crested Grebe), 1961, and traces of her brushstrokes are carried over into the print.
OVERLEAF Unevenness and imprecision can be beautiful: the irregular stripes of Raide (Railway Track), Annika Rimala, 1966 (left) and free rhythm of Nauru (Laugh), Fujiwo Ishimoto, 1981 (right).

ABOVE AND OPPOSITE Rötti, Vuokko Eskolin-Nurmesniemi, 1953. Rötti is an old Finnish dialect word for cotton or linen fabrics much like those used at Marimekko. Designed by hand, these printed stripes preserve something of the spontaneity of handwork.

OPPOSITE AND ABOVE Ukkospilvi (Thundercloud), Fujiwo Ishimoto, 1981. The base fabric showing through a print might ordinarily be considered a fault, but here, as in Nauru, another of Ishimoto's designs (p. 93), it has been utilized as part of the pattern.

COLLABORATION & EXPERIMENTATION

At the beginning, both Printex and Marimekko were seat-of-the-pants operations. In this environment, progress was often the result of trial and error, making Armi and her merry band of printmakers at-times-unwitting iconoclasts. 'I broke all the old rules because I didn't know about them', the founder once said. 'There were so many colours that had never been put together, so many patterns that were too expensive. I didn't know about all those impossibilities, so I tried them anyway.'[14]

This approach is evident in Marimekko's vast archive of sketches, fabric samples and printing tests, which chart the collaborative efforts of artists, designers and the company's print technicians towards a reproducible print design. There may be a single name printed in the selvedge of yardage, but getting from idea to final product is always a team effort, as is exemplified by the back-story of the popular Lumimarja (Snowberry) pattern of 2004, by Erja Hirvi (pp. 100–3), or indeed by the work of not one, but four designers – Hirvi, Maija Louekari, Aino-Maija Metsola and Jenni Tuominen – on the 2019 Ruudut (Squares) pattern (pp. 104–5). Many hands make light work.

ABOVE AND OPPOSITE Putkinotko, Maija Isola, 1957. Isola designed Putkinotko as part of the Luonto (Nature) series, in which real plants were used to create photogram-like prints. The plants were illuminated and then manipulated to design the pattern. Putkinotko features angelica, whose leaves have withered away, leaving behind the stalk and the seedheads.

MARJAPUU

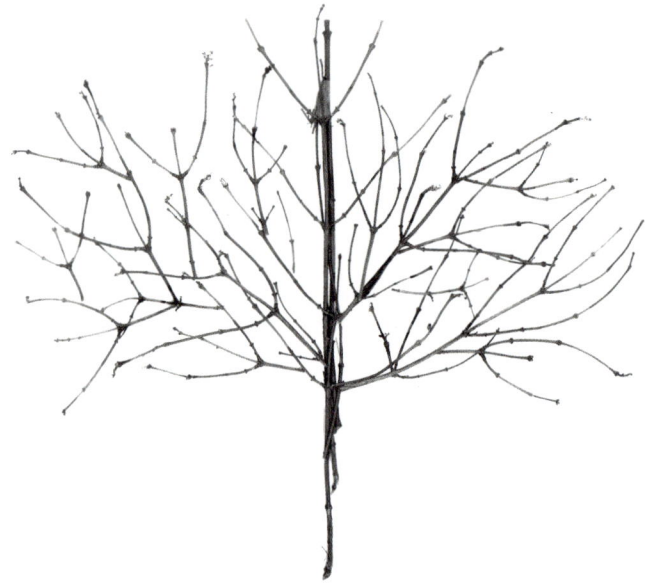

ABOVE, OPPOSITE AND OVERLEAF Erja Hirvi's Lumimarja (Snowberry), 2004, started with a quick sketch on the back of a small paper receipt (left). After submitting her original idea in this form to Marimekko's design director, Hirvi went hunting for cuttings from a live berry tree, and found them, as luck and lore would have it, while stuck in a traffic jam in Helsinki. 'I made a mess with a Xerox machine and spent days on a computer trying to separate berries from lousy colour copies', the designer related in an interview with *Dwell*, 'then Petri Juslin from the Marimekko artwork studio told me to cut the branches and place them in the shape of a tree.'[15] These were scanned (above), and berries were drawn in on the computer. A quick repeat was then made – in just a few hours' time according to Juslin.

ABOVE, RIGHT AND OPPOSITE Ruudut (Squares), 2019, is a collaboration between designers Erja Hirvi, Maija Louekari, Aino-Maija Metsola and Jenni Tuominen. Techniques like paper cutting, in which the mark of the scissor can be detected, were used by Maija Isola to create pattern designs as early as the 1950s (see pp. 86–87), and remain in use decades later, as shown here. The four designers were asked to create abstract, nature-themed interpretations using the paper-cut technique. Each of them created several squares, which were stitched together by Marimekko's artwork studio. These blue and white patterns also seem to reference the work of Henri Matisse.

ABOVE AND OPPOSITE Teippi (Tape), Teija Puranen, 2013. Innovation is as important as iteration at Marimekko. Puranen crafted this bright, abstract pattern by cutting and pasting pieces of adhesive contact paper together. Her original artwork (above) was then translated into a fully reproducible print design by the team at Marimekko.

OVERLEAF Koski (Rapids), Fujiwo Ishimoto, 1986 (left), and Vattenblänk (Water Glitter), Astrid Sylwan, 2010 (right). Even when computers are used to develop patterns, the goal is often to capture the perfectly imperfect aesthetic that was originally achieved through hand-printing.

At Marimekko, meaning is prioritized over mere decoration. The brand was, and to some extent remains, a mirror of its founder. A one-time writer used to confronting a blank page, for Armi, print was a language without words, a form of communication and a path to meaningful connection. A woman with utopian leanings, Armi's belief in the Bauhaus idea of art as a key component of everyday life kept her feet on the ground.

In 2021, Marimekko is to launch an online encyclopedia of prints, Maripedia, with the aim of making all of their vast, expanding archive of patterns accessible to the public. Over 3,500 patterns have been designed since the company's foundation, making it difficult to generalize about their textiles – a result, also, of the many different artists and designers who have been associated with Marimekko over the decades. For every expressionistic design, there is something more subtle or strict, and it is that back and forth, the balancing of opposites, that makes it possible to tease out broad, unifying themes, whether minimal (pp. 128–37) or floral (pp. 150–59), inspired by architecture (pp. 174–83) or nature (pp. 218–27), folklore and storytelling (pp. 196–205) or traditional crafts and decorative arts (pp. 238–47).

Nature is an all-important unifier, at Marimekko and in Finnish culture in general, and it has been conjured by print artists in realistic and abstract ways. Whole collections, such as Aino-Maija Metsola's Sääpäiväkirja (Weather Diary, pp. 228–37), have been built around the Finnish landscape and love of the outdoors. Unikko is just one example of a figurative print; in other, more rigid designs Armi saw 'the geometrics of the earth.'[1] Sometimes, the elements of nature in a design are indicated less by the pattern than by its title. Two such examples are Fujiwo Ishimoto's checkerboard-like Maisema (Landscape) of 1982 and Maija Isola's dotty Kivet (Stones) of 1956.

These patterns have, since Marimekko's beginnings, been translated across dresses, shirts, curtains and tableware. They are made to be lived

'Why dirty up a piece of white cloth unless you have something to say?'[2]

Armi Ratia

'Marimekko is for women whose way of wearing clothes is to forget what they have on.'[4]

Eugenia Sheppard, New York Herald Tribune

with every day. The brand's focus on timeless, empowering design is perhaps epitomized by its dresses (pp. 138–49); many of its early silhouettes are now sought-after vintage pieces. 'Marimekko' is, after all, Finnish for 'Mary's Dress'.

As well as creating collections in-house, Marimekko has also collaborated with companies including Manolo Blahnik, Clinique, Converse, Uniqlo and H&M to bring its patterns to new audiences. Marimekko's own garments are known for their natural, uncomplicated style, made to last and similar in spirit to their print designs. A number of Marimekko designers, including Vuokko Eskolin-Nurmesniemi and Annika Rimala, created prints and garments in tandem (see Jokapoika & Piccolo, pp. 184–95 and Tasaraita, pp. 206–17), while other garments and homewares have been created around particular patterns. 'Our clothes must be loose and express movement, they are part of modern interiors and modern life,' said Armi.[3]

OPPOSITE Folk and Slavic elements are combined in Karuselli (Carousel), Katsuji Wakisaka, 1973.

ICONIC PRINTS

'Marimekko was loose and its battle-cry was freedom',[5] enthused one American journalist in 1972, identifying the qualities that define the company's most iconic prints.

If there is a commonality among the most popular prints, it is a strong graphic identity, whether rendered in bold strokes, like Oona (p. 127) and Joonas (pp. 118–19), or in chiaroscuro, like Selänne or Kuuskajaskari (p. 234). It is not uncommon for prints to be stretched on frames and hung like an artwork.

This blurring of lines between fine and decorative art, graphic and textile design, can be seen as an extension of the multidisciplinary Bauhaus approach; the direct appeal of the most signature prints can be traced back to Armi, a master wordsmith who approached a length of cloth as she might a piece of white paper in a typewriter. The company logo is in fact an easy-to-read variant of the Olivetti typewriter font.

The Marimekko name is known the world over, and its most iconic prints are those that have universal appeal at the same time as being deeply rooted in Finland. 'There must be absolute honesty of design. We look neither to the East nor to the West for inspiration, but try to express something characteristically Finnish', said Armi. 'Finland being a modern country, good design of this type could open possibilities for marketing abroad because our design would have universal appeal.'[6]

ABOVE Unikko (Poppy), Maija Isola, 1964.
OPPOSITE Maija Isola's Kaivo (Well) pattern from 1964, used as a tablecloth, with Oiva (Excellent) ceramics.

OPPOSITE Joonas (Jonah), Maija Isola, 1961.
ABOVE A Joonas curtain in Isola's home on
Rauhankatu Street, Helsinki. Her Nooa (Noah)
pattern, 1961, is visible through the doorway.
LEFT Joonas fabric used as a covering for
the Finnish furniture designer Torsten 'Totti'
Laakso's Kameleontti (Chameleon) sofa, 1966.

OPPOSITE An in-store fitting of Annika Rimala's Ryppypeppu (Wrinkle Behind) jumpsuit, in her 1965 Iso Suomu (Big Fish Scale) print.
ABOVE Four colour-ways of Pikku Suomu (Small Fish Scale), a Rimala design from 1965.
OVERLEAF Isot Kivet (Big Stones), Maija Isola, 1959 (left) and Kivet (Stones), Maija Isola, 1956 (right).
ON P. 124 Siirtolapuutarha (City Garden), Maija Louekari, 2009.
ON P. 125 Lokki (Seagull), Maija Isola, 1961.

©MARIMEKKO OYJ SUOMI-FINLAND MAIJA ISOLA 1956 / K.I. 2008 : "KIVET"
100% CO
100% LI CO/LI

ABOVE AND OPPOSITE Oona, Maija Isola, 1968, being hand-screened in its early days, and shown opposite in its original colour-way.

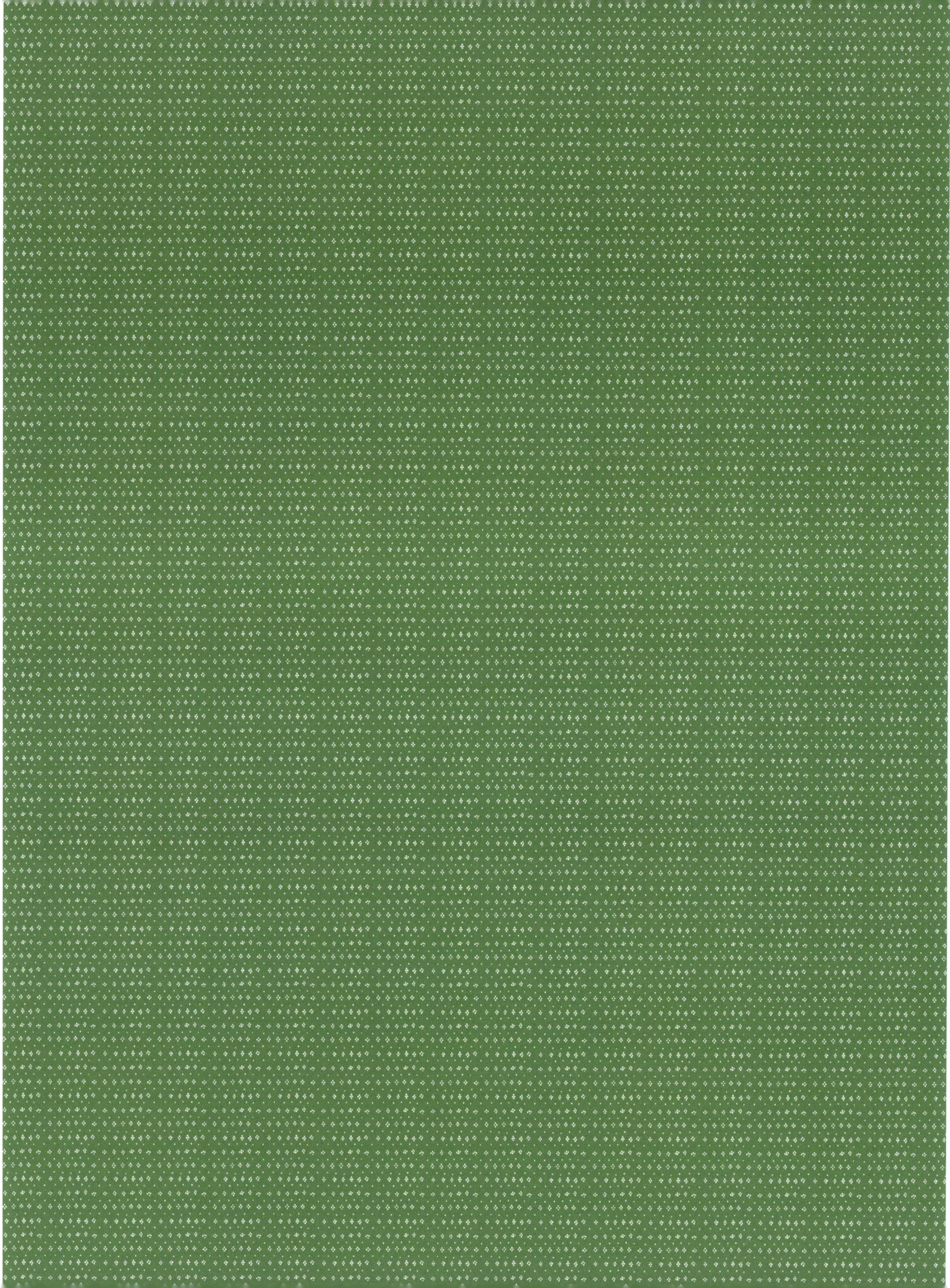

The best-known Marimekko prints might be bold and graphic, but there are many smaller, more delicate patterns in the archive; others may seem plain or even scant, but lend a sense of space and rhythm to garments or homeware. Some of the brand's most impactful prints are made up of seemingly simple motifs and just one or two layers of colour.

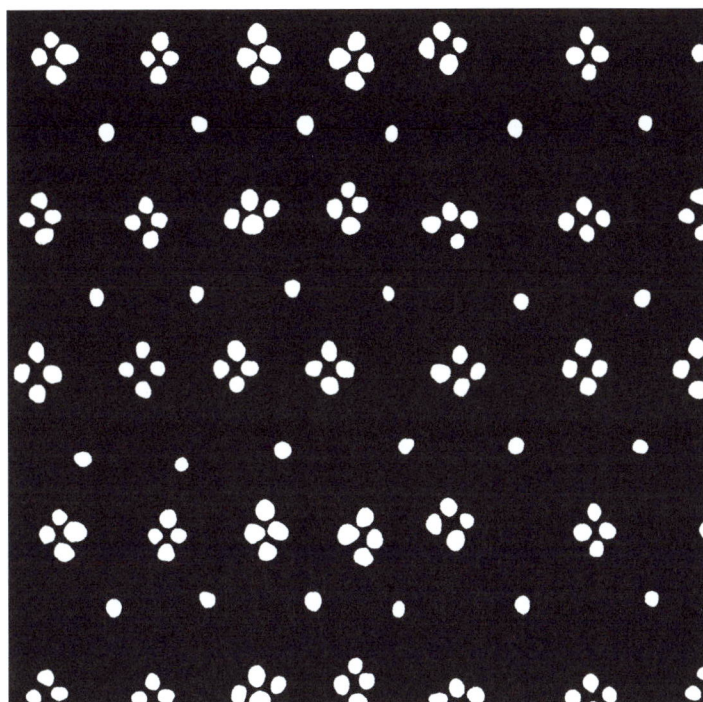

OPPOSITE AND RIGHT Muija (Woman), Maija Isola, 1968.
OVERLEAF Liito (Glide), Maija Isola, 1983 (left) and Nasti, Vuokko Eskolin-Nurmesniemi, 1957 (right).
ON P. 132 Varvunraita (Twig Stripe), Vuokko Eskolin-Nurmesniemi, 1958.
ON P. 133 Pirput Parput, Vuokko Eskolin-Nurmesniemi, 1957.
ON P. 134 Kuiskaus (Whisper), Fujiwo Ishimoto, 1981.
ON P. 135 Tuubiraita (Tube Stripe), Jenni Tuominen, 2017.
ON P. 136 Siluetti (Silhouette), Carina Seth Andersson, 2016.
ON P. 137 Taivas (Sky), Fujiwo Ishimoto, 1985.

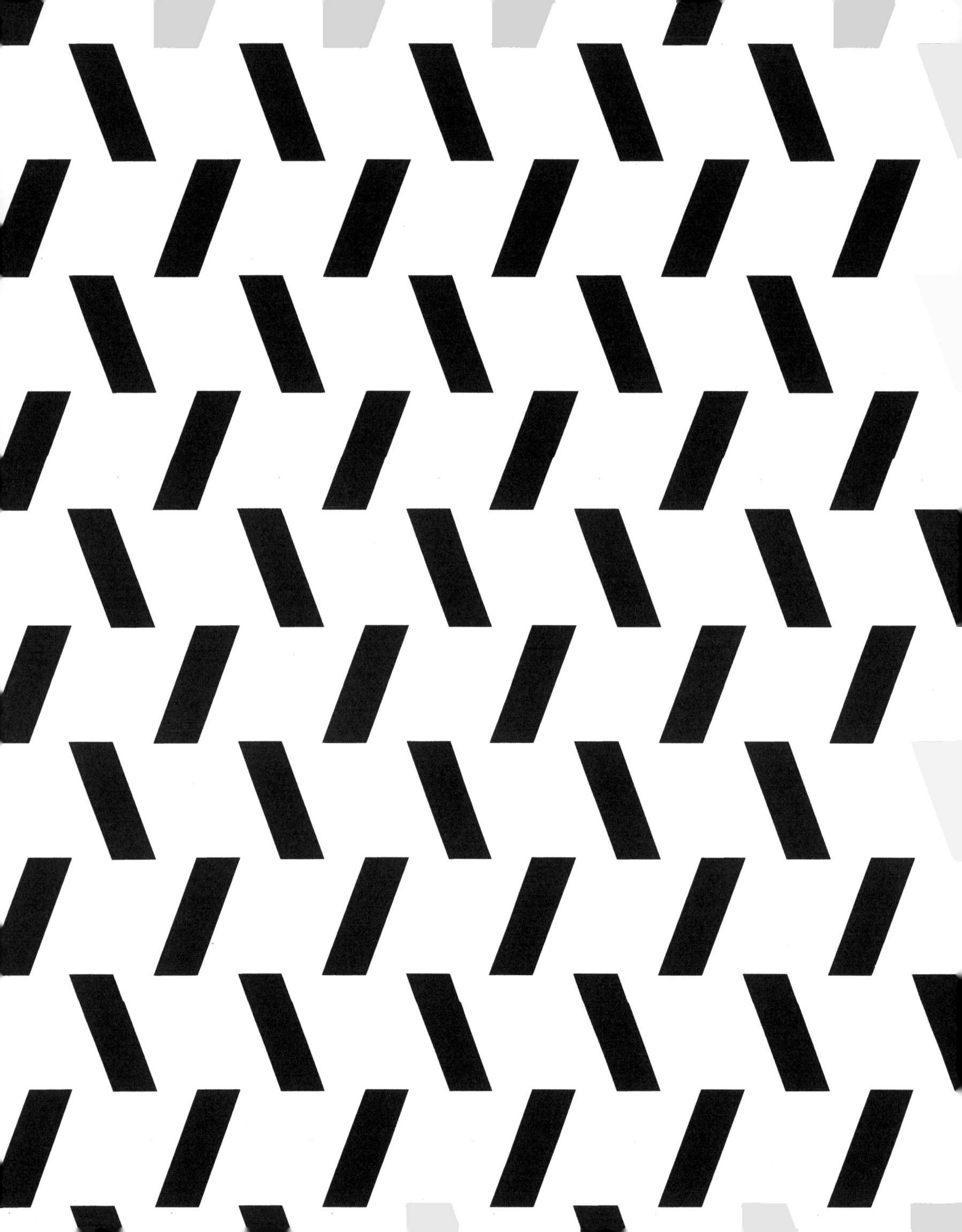

THE DRESS

Although Marimekko clothing has intersected with fashion – particularly in the 1960s and 1970s – Armi always insisted that garments were part of a larger lifestyle concept. She thought of garments in relationship to spaces (natural or architectural), and, always consumed with the idea of home, saw a dress as a sort of house for the body – built to last.

Armi was determined that Marimekko would stand apart from the seasonal and trend-driven fashion industry. Whereas designers may evolve silhouettes and narratives every six months or less, Armi wasn't speaking to a passing moment, but a lasting one. Her goal was to make durable, modern clothes that would never be out of style, and would brighten every day, year after year.

Vuokko Eskolin-Nurmesniemi, who joined the company in 1953, is responsible for many of the designs that made capital-F fashion take notice of Marimekko. She favoured graphic, geometric silhouettes that freed the body, provided comfort and allowed for motion, and designed them for independent women, like Armi and herself, who wanted garments that kept pace with their increasingly liberated lifestyles.

Finland was ahead of the curve on women's rights; some of Eskolin-Nurmesniemi's designs similarly pre-date Parisian developments, though she was after a different end with the 'cookie-cutter' or 'paper doll' silhouette than say, André Courrèges, who popularized it as a Space-Age look. Eskolin-Nurmesniemi designed prints as well as dresses, and this easy A-line shape, that needed no darts, allowed the designer to preserve the integrity of the pattern as much as possible. Marimekko's heavy cottons also adapted well to this geometric shape. Over time, other designers would use materials like knits and corduroy, and would incorporate tailoring and dressmaking techniques into their processes; but the A-line dress has never failed to make the grade, as the flourishing resale market for them shows.

ABOVE Annika Rimala at her desk, photographed by Matti Saanio. Dress sketches, including one for Linjaviitta (Line Sign) and a smocked design are pinned to the wall.
OPPOSITE Annika Rimala's Laine (Wave) design of 1965 was made into this A-line dress in 1966.
OVERLEAF Tony Vaccaro produced many iconic Marimekko images in the 1960s: Anja Vaccaro in New York, wearing a brightly coloured, collared dress designed by Liisa Suvanto (left), and three colour-blocked dresses in the rain (right).

'A woman is sexy, not a dress'[7]

Armi Ratia

OPPOSITE Liisa Suvanto's Korppi (Raven) caftan dress in the Tiet (Roads) print by Katsuji Wakisaka, 1974.
RIGHT Pentti Rinta's Liidokki (Glider) dress in his Kirjo (Spectrum) print, 1973.
OVERLEAF AND ON PP. 146–47 Two designs that have stood the test of time, photographed by Osma Harvilahti in 2020 (left) and Tony Vaccaro in 1965 (right): overleaf, Annika Rimala's Linjaviitta (Line Sign) dress, 1965, made with Vuokko Eskolin-Nurmesniemi's striped Galleria (Gallery) print from 1956, and on pp. 146–47, Liisa Suvanto's Mariessu (Mary's Apron) dress, 1963, in Eskolin-Nurmesniemi's 1953 Piccolo stripe.

ABOVE Annika Rimala's Takila (Rigging) dress, 1967, in Vuokko Eskolin-Nurmesniemi's 1956 Galleria (Gallery) stripe, featured in *Damernas Värld* in 1967.

OPPOSITE A single fruit, plucked from Maija Isola's Päärynä (Pear) print of 1969, on the classic Aikansa shift dress.

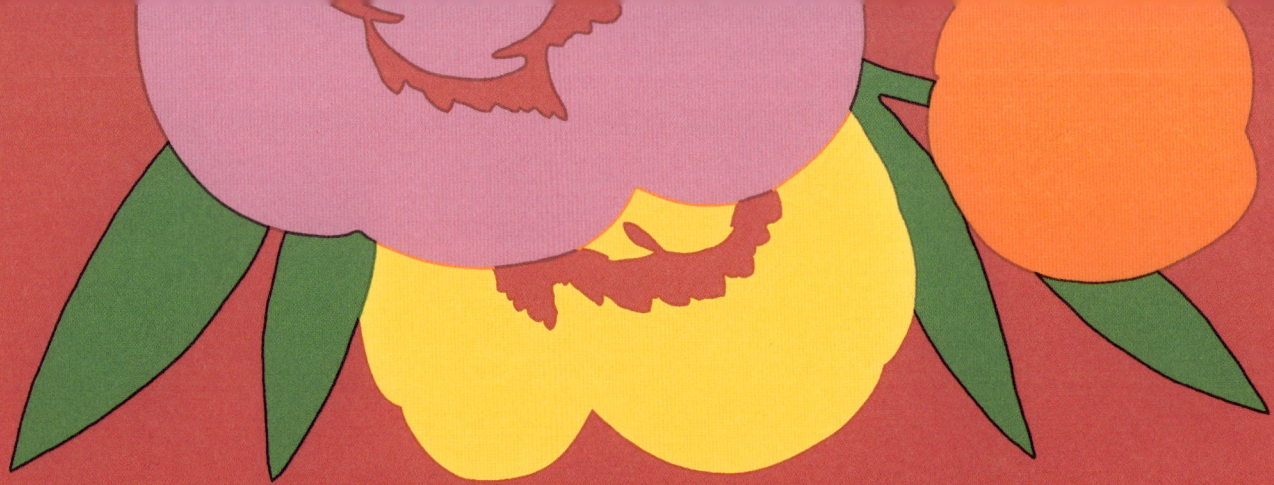

Bouquets, markets and whole fields of flowers have followed Maija Isola's famous poppy (Unikko, pp. 54–73) into the Marimekko archive, which now ranges from unruly, exuberant blooms to the simplest posies. Marimekko's flowers do not aim to compete with nature, but to reinterpret and complement its beauty and variety.

OPPOSITE Kuuma (Hot), Fujiwo Ishimoto, 1978.
BELOW Vikuri (Unruly), Erja Hirvi, 2018.
OVERLEAF Primavera (Spring), Maija Isola, 1972 (left), and Kasvio (Flora), Lotta Maija, 2018 (right).
ON P. 154 Puketti (Bouquet), Annika Rimala, 1965.
ON P. 155 Kukkaketo (Flower Field), Fujiwo Ishimoto, 1975.
ON P. 156 Kukkatori (Flower Market), Maija Isola, 1970.
ON P. 157 Mehiläinen (Bee), Maija Isola, 1973.
ON P. 158 Juhannustaika (Midsummer Spell), Aino-Maija Metsola, 2007.
ON P. 159 Viivakukka (Line Flower), Satu Maaranen, 2016.

POP PRINTS

Printmaking has always been elevated to an art form at Marimekko, and just as the brand's garments have occasionally intersected with the fashion industry, so have its prints been in dialogue with the fine arts. One such meeting was with the Pop and Op Art movements. The former broke with tradition and hierarchy by pulling references and imagery from popular culture; the latter destabilized the viewer through optical illusions.

Marimekko dresses, designed for everyday wear, were aligned with the democratic spirit of Pop beyond their shared, brilliant colour palette. Some of its patterns, among them Kaarina Kellomäki's Linssi (Lens, pp. 172–73), 1966, Annika Rimala's Kruuna (Heads), 1967 and Klaava (Tails), 1967, and Maija Isola's Melooni (Melon, pp. 170–71), 1963, were aligned with Op's teasing graphics. As with the sack dress, Armi and co. were early on this trend, and Marimekkos in these artful styles hold their own alongside work by designers like Rudi Gernreich, a major proponent of the Mod look, and the print-centric Italian designer Emilio Pucci.

ABOVE, OPPOSITE AND OVERLEAF Keidas (Oasis), Annika Rimala, 1967, made into the Monrepos dress, 1967 (above), and the Fortuuna mini shift dress (opposite).
ON P. 164 Jokeri (Joker), Annika Rimala, 1967.
ON P. 165 Tarha (Garden), Annika Rimala, 1963, made into the Rakkauskirje dress.

OPPOSITE Laine (Wave), Annika Rimala, 1965, especially well-suited to a ruched bathing suit, 1960s.
ABOVE Iso Laine (Big Wave), Annika Rimala, 1965.
OVERLEAF Seireeni (Siren), Maija Isola, 1964 (left), and Petrooli (Petroleum), Annika Rimala, 1963 (right).

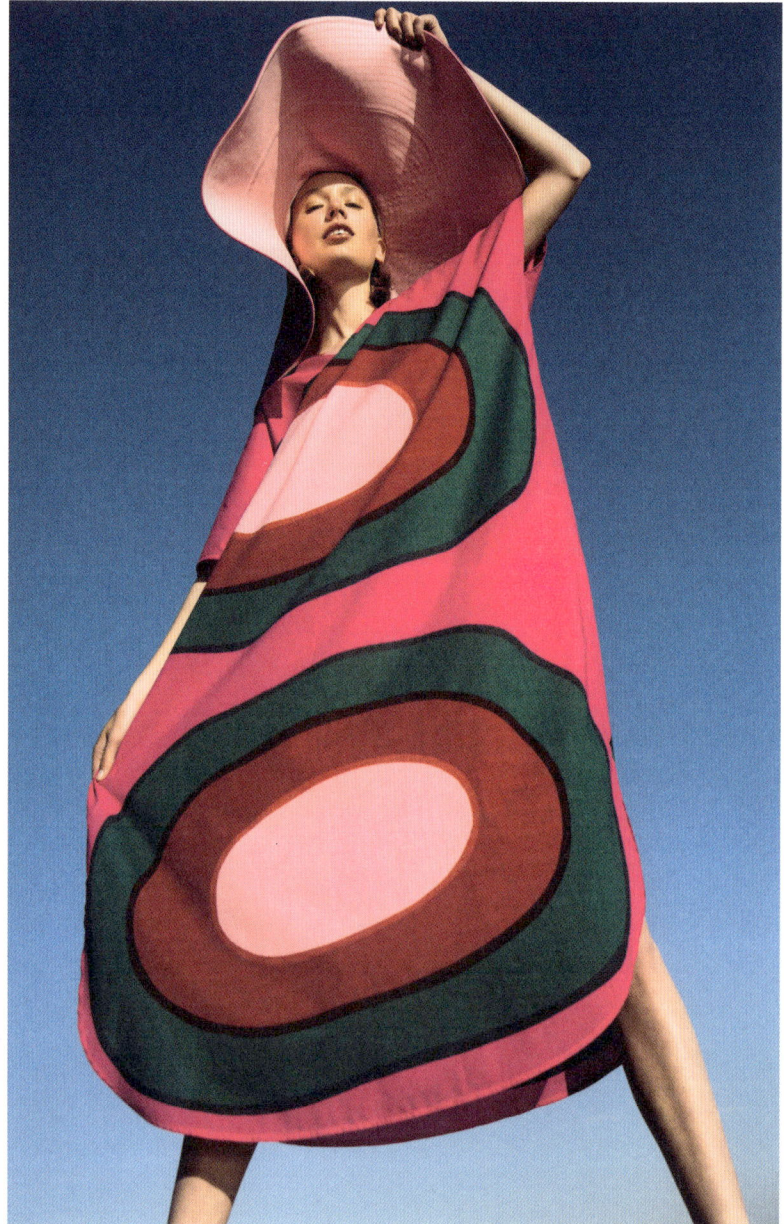

ABOVE AND OPPOSITE Melooni (Melon), Maija Isola, 1963, made into the Rantaloma (Beach Holiday) kaftan (above right).
OVERLEAF Linssi (Lens), Kaarina Kellomäki, 1966, and Finnish model Ninja Sarasalo in a Linssi-patterned dress and hat designed by Mika Piirainen, 2003.

Alvar Aalto, Eero Saarinen, Aarno Ruusuvuori: Finland has produced numerous iconic architects, and the Finnish love for architecture is well-known worldwide. The colours, shapes and materials of the built environment – in Marimekko's home city of Helsinki and elsewhere – have served as a starting point for Marimekko's designers (including its founder, see Tiiliskivi, pp. 178–79 and Faruk, p. 183) since the brand's very beginnings.

OPPOSITE Tiibet (Tibet), Vuokko Eskolin-Nurmesniemi, 1953.
RIGHT Ikkuna (Window), Pentti Rinta, 1969.
OVERLEAF Kukko ja Kana (Rooster and Hen), Maija Isola, 1965 (left), and Kalasääski (Osprey), Maija Isola, 1962 (right).
ON PP. 178–79 Tiiliskivi (Brick), Armi Ratia, 1952.
ON P. 180 Frekvenssi (Frequency), Harri Koskinen, 2006.
ON P. 181 Ruutukaava (Grid Pattern), Maija Louekari, 2008.
ON P. 182 Keisarinkruunu (Emperor's Crown), Maija Isola, 1966.
ON P. 183 Faruk, Armi Ratia, 1952.

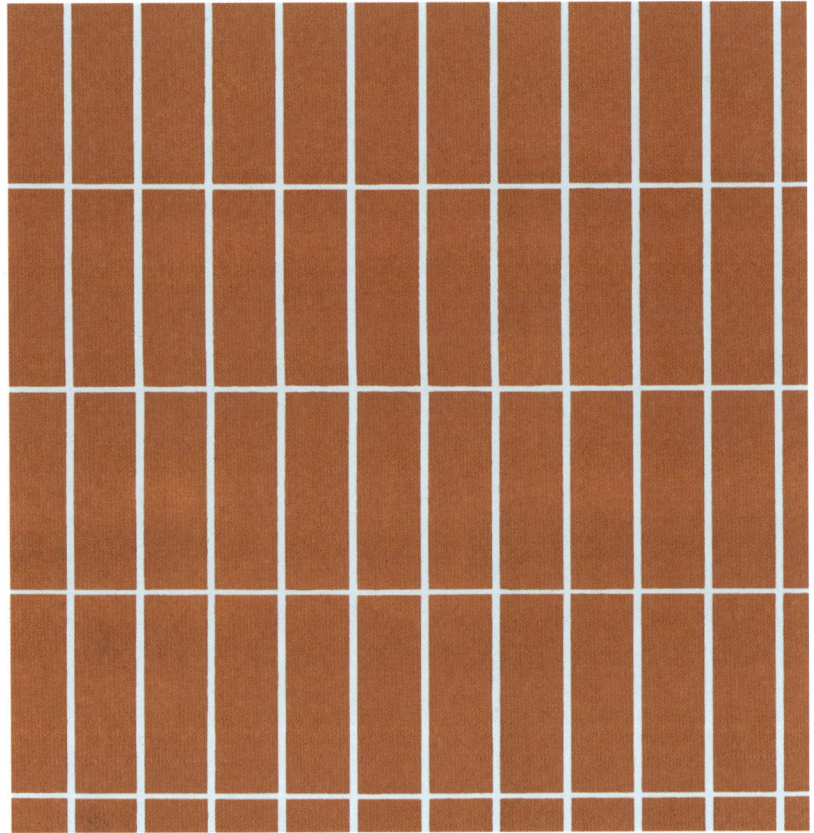

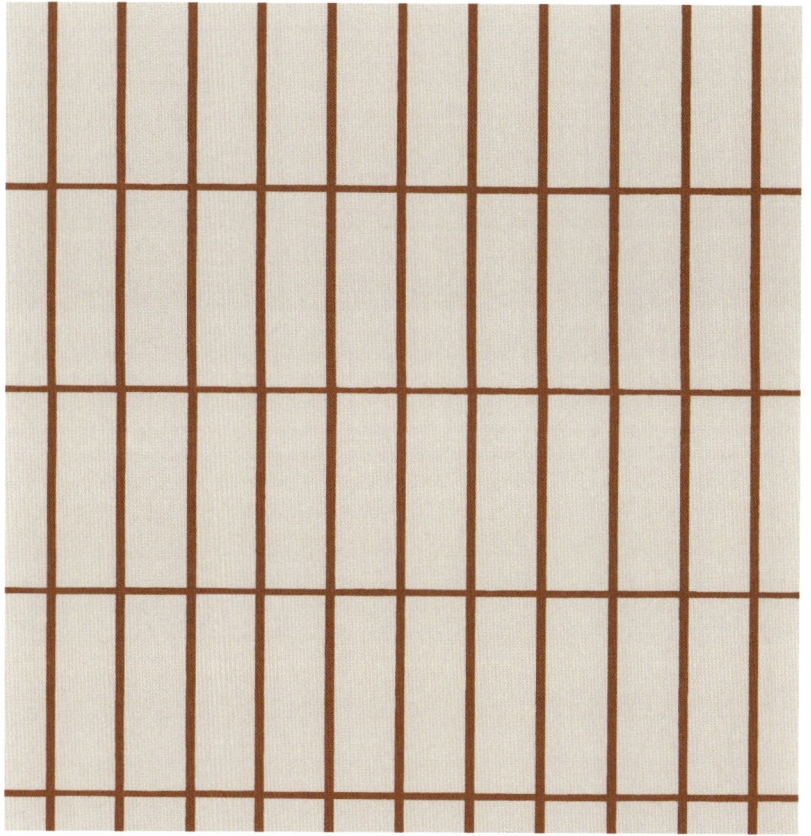
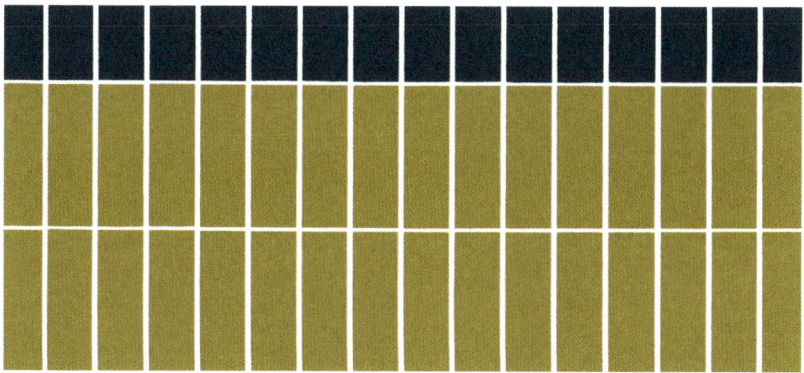

JOKAPOIKA
& PICCOLO

Soon after she joined Marimekko, Vuokko Eskolin-Nurmesniemi had her first big 'win' with a hand-drawn stripe called Piccolo. Small but mighty, this print has never gone out of production, and neither has the Jokapoika (Every Boy) shirt that she fashioned from it, which became Mari's playmate in 1956.

Based on the design of a Finnish farmer's shirt, Jokapoika was Marimekko's first men's garment, though it has always worked as a gender-neutral design.[8] It has been called 'a uniform for the creative',[9] and 'the architect's shirt',[10] and there are photographs of Benjamin Thompson, founder of Design Research, through which Marimekko was introduced to America, wearing his version. Like Armi, who Thompson once suggested was 'possibly the most important female influence in contemporary design',[11] the architect believed in the meeting of form and function: 'For art to be part of our life we must live with it, not just go to museums'.[12]

Eskolin-Nurmesniemi painted Piccolo's stripe by hand, rendering them perfectly imperfect. Minna Kemell-Kutvonen, Marimekko's Director of Home Design and Prints, explains that in order to ensure that the cotton ground wouldn't show through, overlaps were used intentionally. The result was the creation of a 'new, surprising, third colour.' This proved to be such a tempting opportunity to play with palettes that about 1,000 different colour-ways have been made throughout the years.

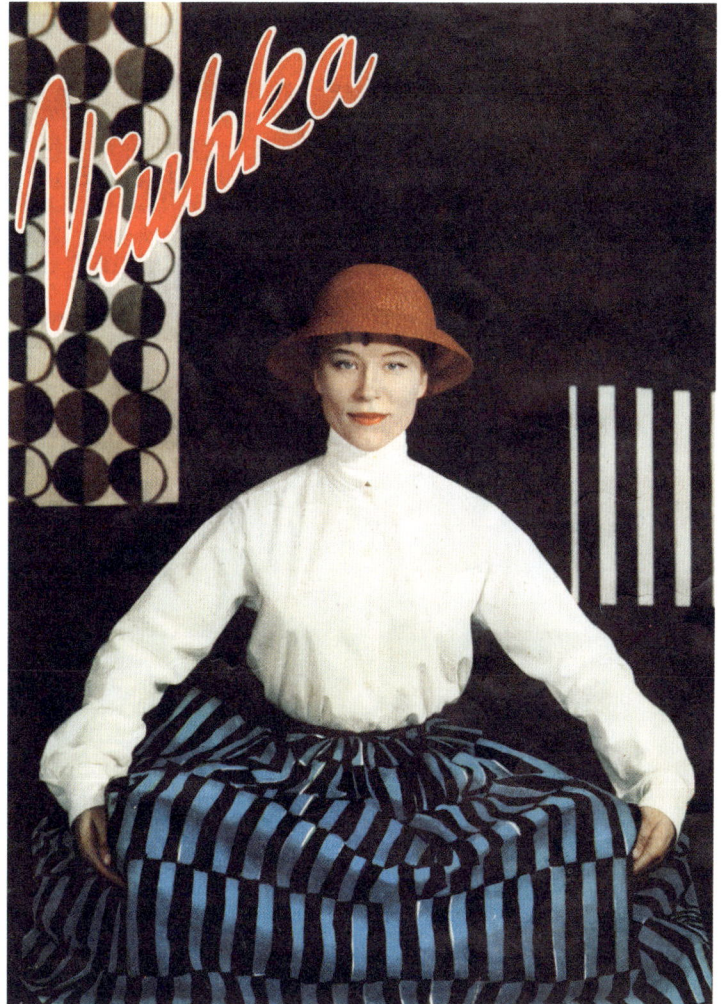

OPPOSITE Chawntell Kulkarni, Elsa Sjökvist and Jenny Sinkaberg, photographed by David Luraschi in variations of the Piccolo stripe, Spring/Summer 2020.
ABOVE Vuokko Eskolin-Nurmesniemi created a multitude of stripes in her time at Marimekko, among them Pohjanakka (a character in the Kalevala epic), 1954, shown here on the cover of *Viuhka* magazine in 1954, Rötti (p. 94), Raituli (a playful variation on the Finnish word for stripe), 1956, and Kukkaraita (Flower Stripe), 1959.

LEFT AND ABOVE Georgia O'Keeffe and her dogs photographed by Todd Webb in her garden at Abiquiú, New Mexico, in about 1962. O'Keeffe is wearing her Äidin takki (Mother's Coat) smock, shown above with its sash, in Vuokko Eskolin-Nurmesniemi's 1953 Ristipiccolo stripe.
OPPOSITE Piccolo, Vuokko Eskolin-Nurmesniemi, 1953.
OVERLEAF Armi Ratia in a Jokapoika shirt, with a model in another of Marimekko's stripes, outside the brand's earlier printing location on Vanha Talvitie, Helsinki.

OPPOSITE AND ABOVE Piccolo, Vuokko Eskolin-Nurmesniemi,
1953, in a few of its hundreds of colour-ways.
OVERLEAF Folded Jokapoika shirts (left) and a tunic from pre-Fall
2016 (right) display even more shades of Piccolo.

OPPOSITE Piccolo, Vuokko Eskolin-Nurmesniemi, 1953.
ABOVE Model in a pastel Jokapoika, Spring/Summer 2020.

Playful and fun without being naive, Armi's particular brand of utopianism is evident in the brilliantly coloured scenes and cast of vibrant animals, fruits and figures that have made their way into many Marimekko prints. Their visual storytelling is often heightened by the titles printed in the margins: Veljekset (Brothers, p. 198) celebrates a century of Finnish independence with fantastical images of its flora and fauna, while Max ja Moritz (Max and Moritz, p. 204) conjures up the popular, rhyming children's story of two naughty little boys. And who is HO-HOI! calling out to?

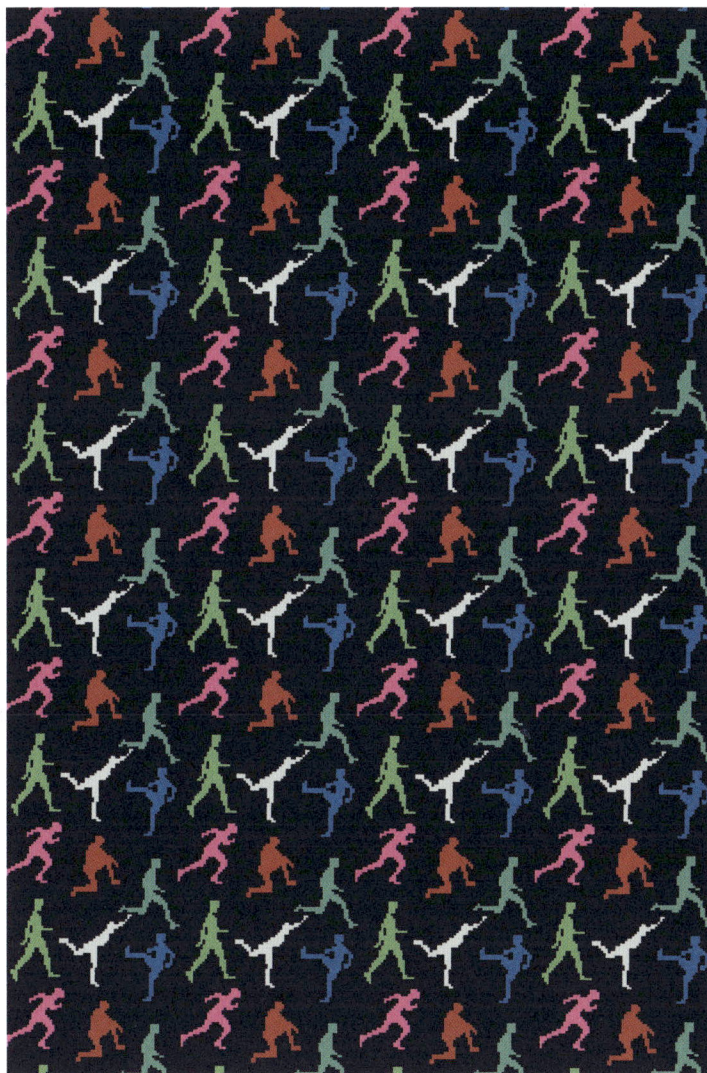

OPPOSITE HO-HOI! (HEY THERE!), Maija Louekari, 2004.
RIGHT Kenttä (Field), Fujiwo Ishimoto, 1985.
OVERLEAF Veljekset (Brothers), Maija Louekari, 2016 (left), and Ketunmarja (Fox Berry), Aino-Maija Metsola, 2018 (right).
ON P. 200 Kaksoset (Twins), Maija Isola, 1970.
ON P. 201 Appelsiini (Orange), Maija Isola, 1950.
ON P. 202 Päärynä (Pear), Maija Isola, 1969.
ON P. 203 Pepe, Maija Isola, 1970.
ON P. 204 Max ja Moritz (Max and Moritz), Maija Isola, 1968.
ON P. 205 Charles, Maija Isola, 1973.

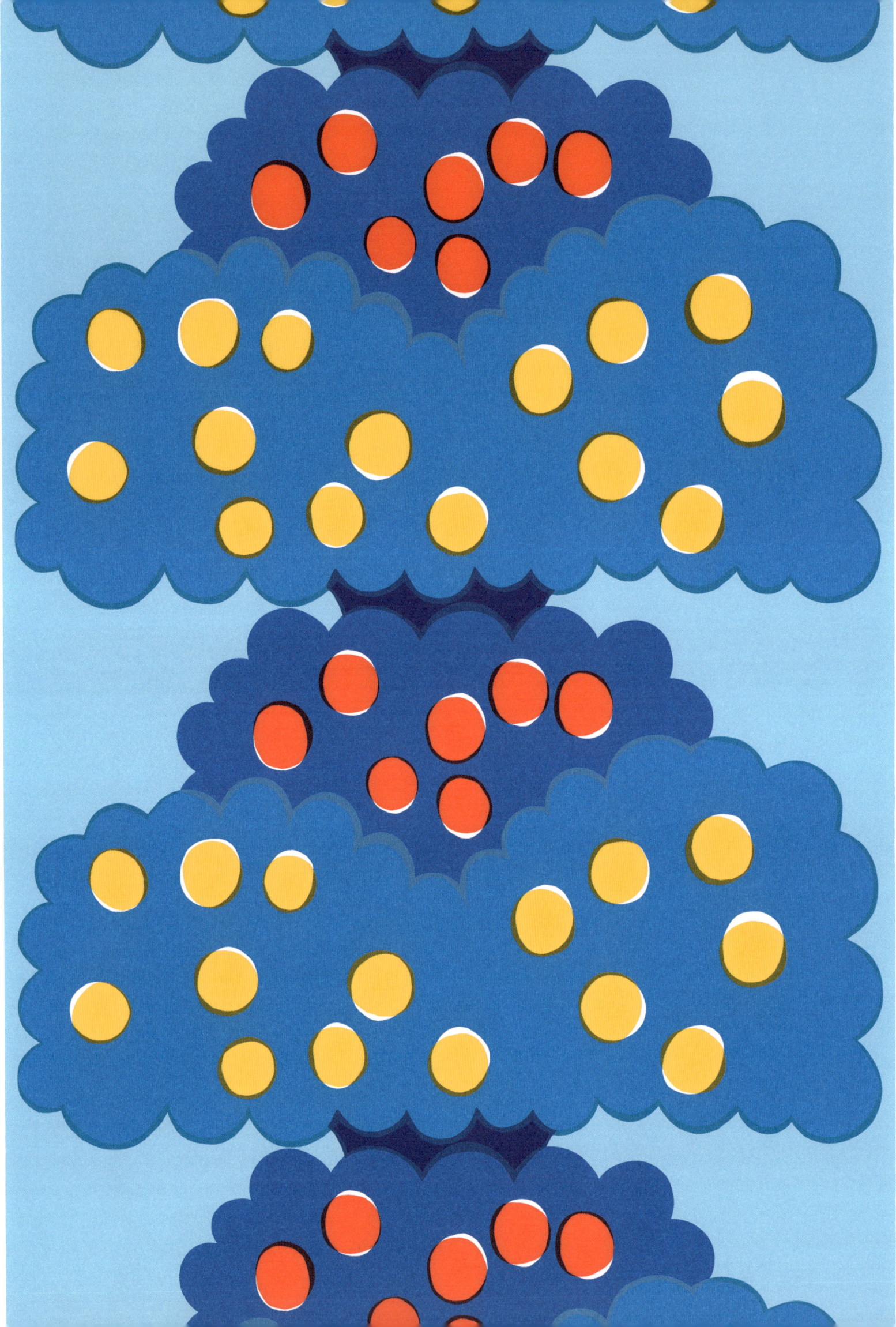

Charles
7.4.73
Maija Isola
Ain-el-Turc

TASARAITA

Like Vuokko Eskolin-Nurmesniemi, the charismatic Annika Rimala also left her mark on Marimekko with stripes – and was, among her other innovations, the first to use knit fabrics at the company.

Piccolo's hand-drawn lines accommodated a degree of randomness; Rimala called her own winning stripe design Tasaraita (Even Stripe). Because it is woven into soft knits that conform to the body, Tasaraita also has an element of flexibility. Designed to be worn with jeans, a symbol of youth culture, Tasaraita shirts were aligned with the liberated spirit of 1968. The pattern, which is visually on the straight and narrow, comes with an open-minded and inclusive message. The even stripes signify equality and acceptance: from the beginning, Tasaraita shirts were designed to be unisex. In recent years, Marimekko has used the Tasaraita pattern as an expression of its solidarity with the LGBTQ+ community, reimagining the stripes in rainbow colours.

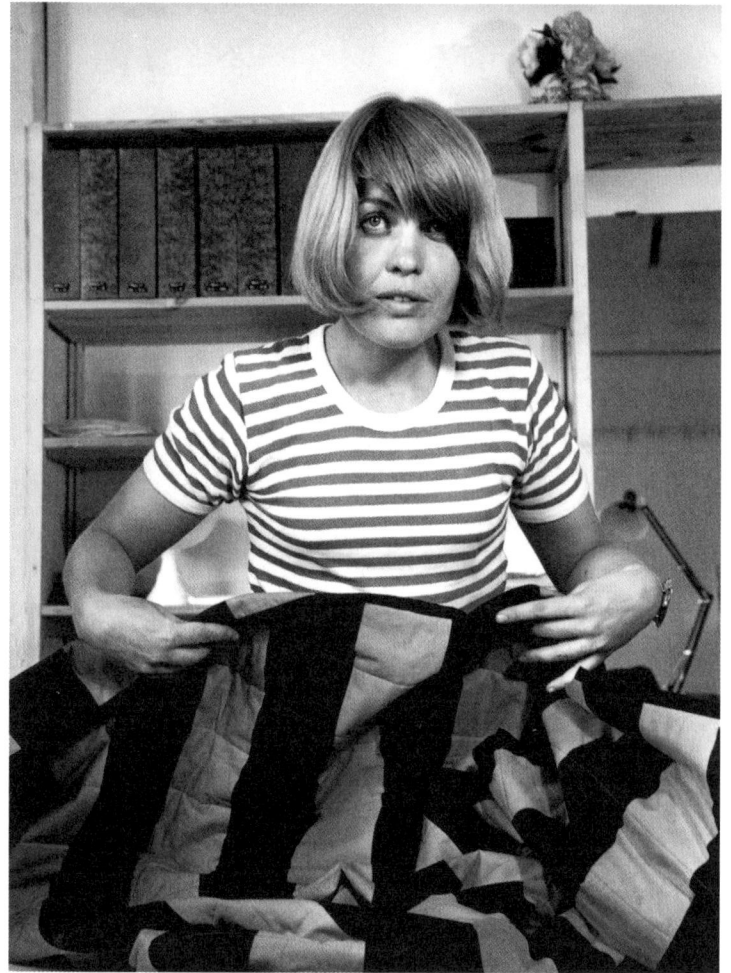

ABOVE Annika Rimala in her Tasaraita (Even Stripe) t-shirt.
OPPOSITE Variants of Tasaraita, Annika Rimala, 1968.
OVERLEAF Stripes galore – in the 1960s and 2020.

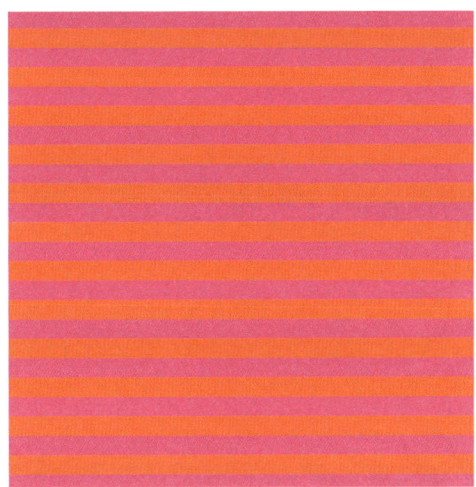

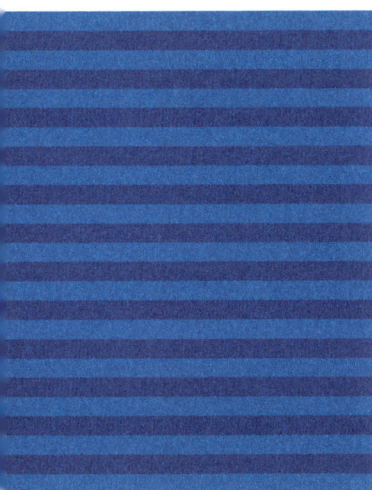

Even stripes for equality.

OPPOSITE Even stripes for equality: Tasaraita in support of LGBTQ+ rights, 2020.
ABOVE A stripy Goth (left); matching stripes for a hairdo and bag (right).
OVERLEAF A unisex design from its very beginnings, Tasaraita has proven adaptable for many silhouettes and occasions.

ABOVE AND OPPOSITE Photographs showing Marimekko printers
working in Tasaraita stripes in the 1970s and in 2020 suggest that
they have become the unofficial Marimekko uniform.

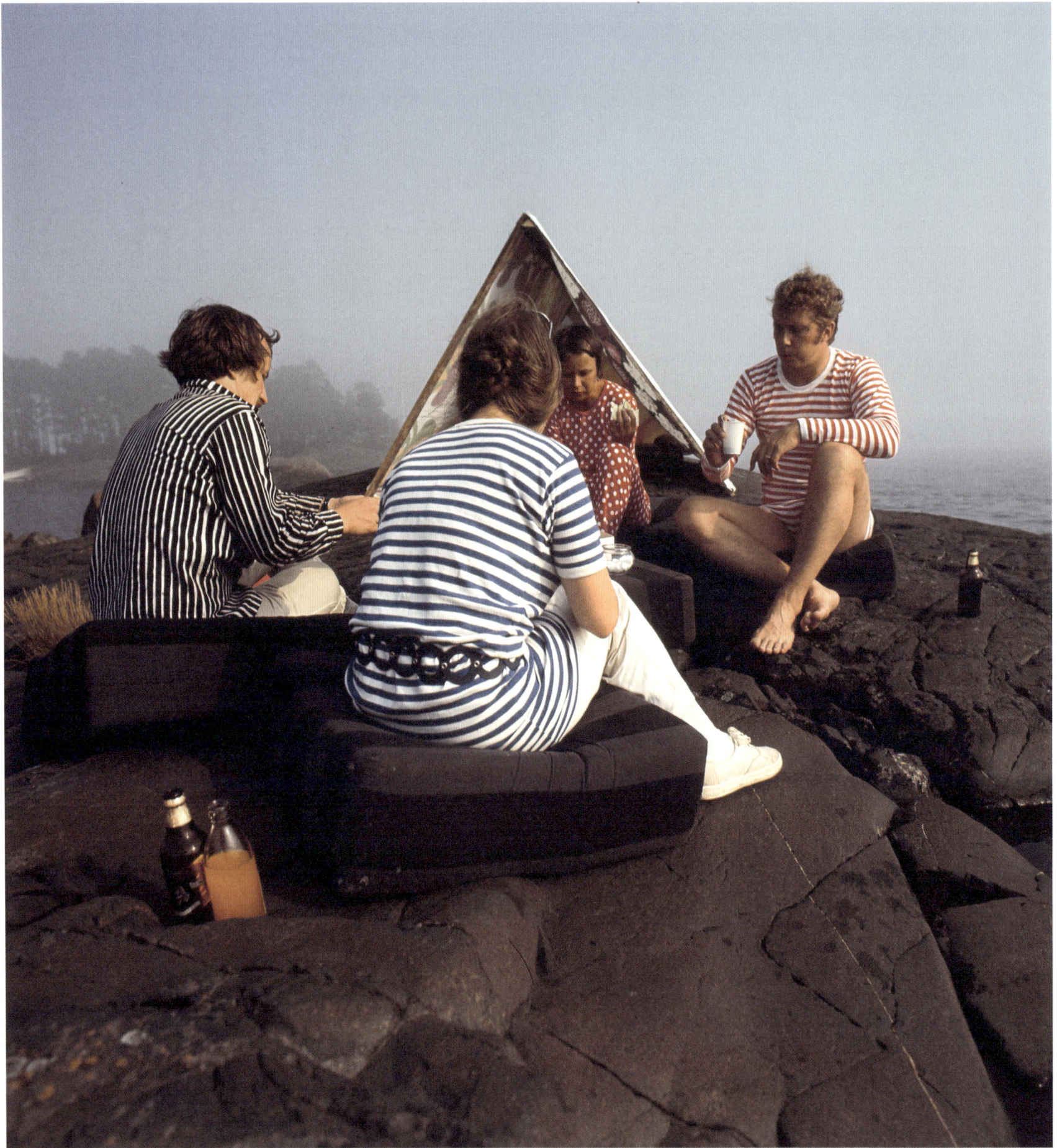

ABOVE AND OPPOSITE Stripes are right for life in the wild, photographed by Claire Aho in the 1970s – or in a family room in the 2010s.

A love of nature has been at the core of Marimekko from the start – from the details of flora and fauna to landscapes, weather systems and the seasons. Many different moments and forms of nature are represented in the brand's pattern archives. Designers have also sought to capture something of the movement and feel of the natural world in cloth, resulting in many of Marimekko's organic, impressionistic designs.

OPPOSITE Kesanto (Fallow), Fujiwo Ishimoto, 1988.
RIGHT Maisema (Landscape), Fujiwo Ishimoto, 1982.
OVERLEAF Tuuli (Wind), Maija Isola, 1971 (left), and Uimari (Swimmer), Maija Isola, 1969 (right).
ON P. 222 Joiku (traditional Sámi song), Aino-Maija Metsola, 2008.
ON P. 223 Harmaja (Sääpäiväkirja/Weather Diary collection), Aino-Maija Metsola, 2012.
ON P. 224 Suuri Taiga (Great Taiga), Fujiwo Ishimoto, 1993.
ON P. 225 Lepo (Rest), Fujiwo Ishimoto, 1991.
ON P. 226 Lainehtiva (Undulating) and Salava (Crack Willow), both Fujiwo Ishimoto, 1988.
ON P. 227 Poronjäkälä (Reindeer Lichen), Aino-Maija Metsola, 2018.

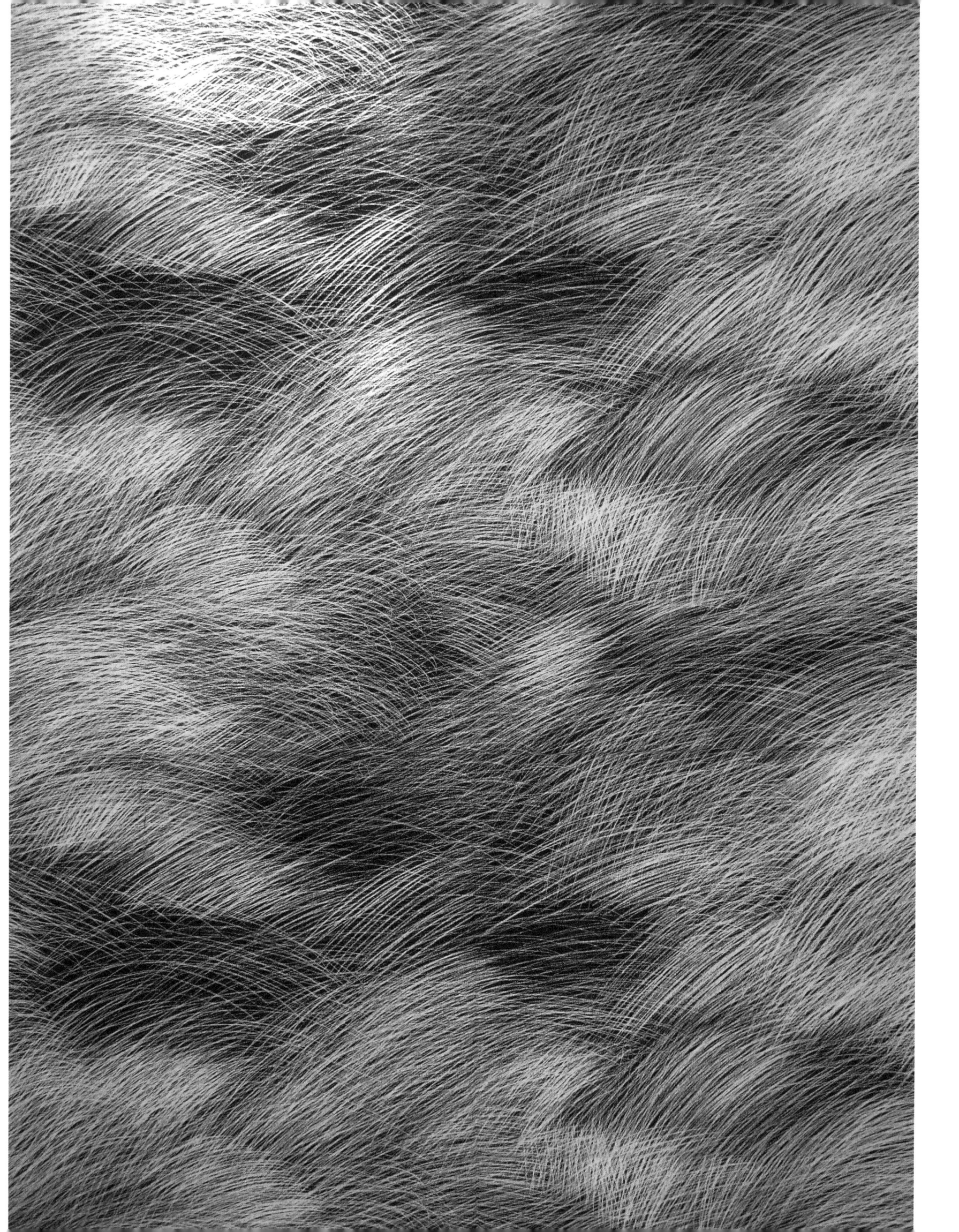

WEATHER DIARY

Nature plays an important role in Finnish culture, which is traditionally agricultural. Seasons, for example, are often marked with the changing of curtains and other home textiles. The elements are a recurring motif in Marimekko designs, but the artist and designer Aino-Maija Metsola took this theme in a wholly new direction when she designed the Sääpäiväkirja (Weather Diary) prints, based on artworks she created over several months in 2012, from her home on a Finnish island. The prints were developed from aquarelle paintings, which are softer and more atmospheric than graphic.

Sääpäiväkirja is unique in the specificity and interconnectedness of its narrative. This was not a musing on colour or object or style, but a personal documentation of specific places and weather patterns in Finland. Each pattern takes its name from an island in the Finnish archipelago, many of which Metsola had visited on sailing trips. The patterns were translated across posters, fabrics, home textiles and Sami Ruotsalainen's Oiva (Excellent) ceramics.

ABOVE Oiva/Sääpäiväkirja (Weather Diary) jug.
OPPOSITE Artworks relating to the Sääpäiväkirja prints, aquarelle and pen, 2012.

OPPOSITE Jussarö, Aino-Maija
Metsola, 2012.
RIGHT AND BELOW Sääpäiväkirja
diary, coffee cup and artwork related
to the Jussarö pattern.
OVERLEAF Luovi (Tack), Aino-Maija
Metsola, 2014, in two colour-ways.

OPPOSITE Kuuskajaskari, Aino-Maija Metsola, 2012.
ABOVE AND OVERLEAF A mix of Oiva/Sääpäiväkirja, Oiva/
Räsymatto (Rag Rug) and Oiva/Siirtolapuutarha (City Garden)
tableware makes a beautiful table setting, with Kuuskajaskari
fabric used as a tablecloth.

The cavalcade of exuberant, densely patterned designs in Marimekko's archive offers a true counterpoint to the brand's more minimal creations (see pp. 128–37). Influenced by Finland's location between East and West, patterns are inspired by Scandinavian and Slavic crafts and design traditions, folklore and the decorative arts. Lanketti (Form, p. 245) simplifies the scallop motif dressed up in Satula (Saddle, p. 240) to a clean, graphic form, found also in Papajo (Papaya, p. 244), which takes inspiration from further afield: Annika Rimala created the pattern after seeing Maya carvings in Mexico.

OPPOSITE Tulipunainen (Scarlet), Maija Isola, 1960.
ABOVE Amfora (Amphora), Maija Isola, 1949.
OVERLEAF Satula (Saddle), Maija Isola, 1960 (left), and Tantsu (Dance), Maija Isola, 1960 (right).
ON P. 242 Raakel (Rachel), Paavo Halonen, 2014.
ON P. 243 Juustomuotti (Cheese Mould), Paavo Halonen, 2017.
ON P. 244 Papajo (Papaya), Annika Rimala, 1968.
ON P. 245 Lanketti (Form), Annika Rimala, 1965.
ON P. 246 Ananas (Pineapple), Maija Isola, 1962.
ON P. 247 Fandango, Maija Isola, 1962.

© MARIMEKKO OYJ SUOMI-FINLAND PAAVO HALONEN 2017: "JUUSTOMUOTTI"

SURFACE PATTERN

In 1960, Armi told an Associated Press reporter that she had 'other products than ready-to-wear always dropping from my head.'[13] Almost fifty years later, Sami Ruotsalainen, a graduate of the University of Art and Design Helsinki (now the Aalto University School of Arts, Design and Architecture), was commissioned to translate the Marimekko ethos using pottery, and in 2009 Oiva (Excellent) ceramics were introduced. Notable for its minimal shapes, beautiful in themselves, the collection also nicely frames Marimekko prints.

Ruotsalainen managed to create clean-lined pieces that invite touch, thus retaining the sense of the hand and handicraft that is a part of Marimekko's DNA and speaks to the deep need for comfort that often arises in times of change. 'There is more of a need today for coming back to simplicity', observed Armi in the tumultuous year of 1972, 'I see the need all around – people baking their own bread, handcrafting. It's simplicity and truth unconfused by the complexity of the external world.'[14] As digital technology makes that world more accessible, so the longing for authenticity and human connection grows.

Adding yet more colour and fun to tablescapes is the Sukat Makkaralla (Socks Rolled Down, p. 257) glassware collection, designed by Anu Penttinen in 2010. The hand-blown pieces speak to Marimekko's tradition of 'perfect imperfection' in print design, and also extend the idea of comfort that Armi aimed for when she introduced clothing. That everyday joys are informal and familiar doesn't mean they can't be elevated. 'I think beauty is very necessary,' Armi once said. 'But it's possible to find beauty in the simple things of home rather than in fancy possessions.'[15]

ABOVE Oiva (Excellent) sketches by Sami Ruotsalainen.
OPPOSITE Illustration by Antti Kalevi, showing plant pots with the Räsymatto (Rag Rug) and Primavera (Spring) patterns, 2019.

ABOVE AND OPPOSITE Table settings using pieces
from the Oiva/Unikko collection.

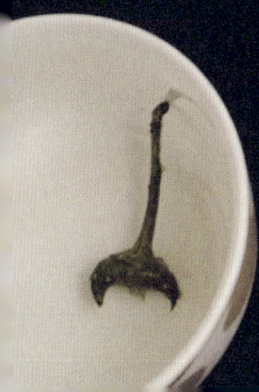

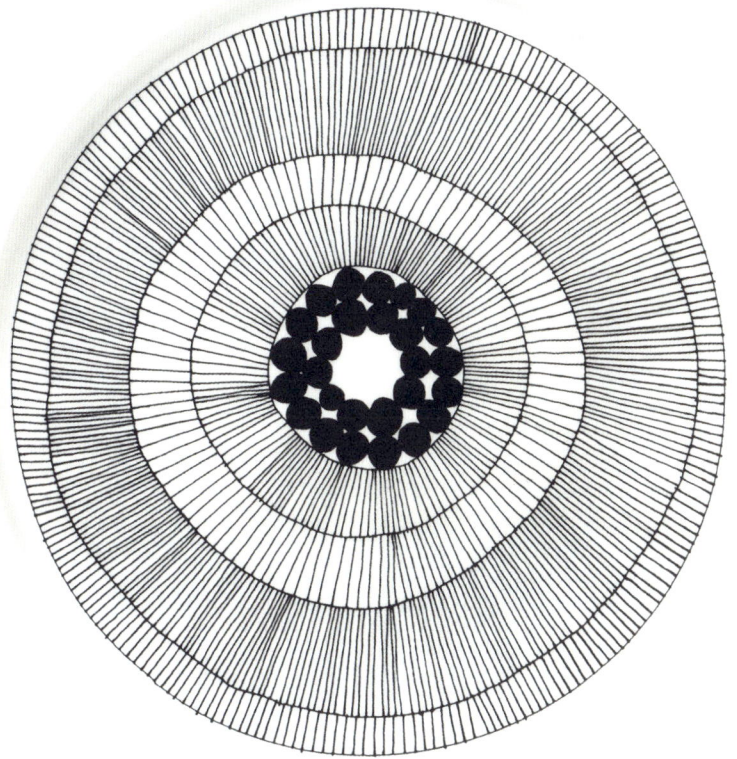

OPPOSITE AND LEFT Four different colour-ways of the allotment-inspired Siirtolapuutarha (City Garden), Maija Louekari, 2009. ABOVE AND BELOW Oiva/Siirtolapuutarha plate and bowl.

ABOVE AND RIGHT An espresso cup with the Räsymatto (Rag Rug) pattern, and two colour-ways of Räsymatto, Maija Louekari, 2009. OPPOSITE Oiva pieces enhance the everyday pleasures of dining: a table setting with Oiva/Räsymatto, Oiva/Siirtolapuutarha and Oiva/Sääpäiväkirja pieces.

OPPOSITE A cupboard with Oiva in Siirtolapuutarha and
Räsymatto patterns.
ABOVE A table setting, complete with Sukat Makkaralla glasses
and Carina Seth Andersson's mouth-blown Flower vase.

4. Marimekko Next

Technological innovations, globalization, a pandemic: none of these major changes have dimmed the happy, can-do, collaborative spirit that animates Marimekko and is the legacy of its founder, Armi Ratia. It is, in fact, something that continues to light the way forward as the company, now seventy years young, charts an increasingly responsible approach to the future.

Long established as an iconic lifestyle brand, as Marimekko enters the 2020s it is increasingly focused on how it can be a better tenant on earth. Sustainability is a top agenda item as the company continues to globalize. Marimekko's commitment to this goal is deep and extensive, considering design, product life cycles, materials, production, supply chains, logistics and governance.

Some of the most exciting developments build on the Finns' famed relationship with nature, and the geographical makeup of Finland itself, which is about seventy-five per cent forest. Since 2013, Marimekko has been working collaboratively with Aalto University and the University of Helsinki

'We really want to be good for the planet'

Sanna-Kaisa Niikko

to develop a biodegradable birch cellulose fibre without the use of dangerous chemicals, through the Ioncell solvent method.[1] In 2020, *Fast Company* magazine recognized Marimekko's innovative work with the Finnish company Spinnova, who have developed technology that spins wood pulp into a biodegradable textile fibre without harmful chemicals, using about ninety-nine per cent less water than is needed for cotton production. The first prototype garments made using the fibre, designed by Marimekko's ready-to-wear designer Riikka Buri, naturally featured the classic Unikko (Poppy) print (see p. 263). Marimekko's pre-Fall 2021 collection includes pieces printed with natural plant-derived indigo dye (opposite), extracted from Finnish woad – the result of a collaboration with Natural Indigo Finland, begun in 2019. In-house, designers have been working with leftover cotton fabrics to make new, patchwork products (see p. 266).

Sustainability is also firmly woven into the company values through its commitment to timeless designs that exist outside the trend cycle. In high-quality fabrics with contemporary silhouettes, Marimekko garments are built to last and be passed on. Proof of concept is to be found in the flourishing collector's market for vintage Marimekkos.

Company President and CEO Tiina Alahuhta-Kasko traces the sustainability of Marimekko products 'from their timeless, empowering aesthetic as well as their durability and longevity' back to the company's

PREVIOUS SPREAD From left: Ostjakki (Khanty), Fujiwo Ishimoto, 1983; Käpykukka (Pinecone Flower), Carina Seth Andersson, 2019; Louhi and Hyhmä (Frost), both Aino-Maija Metsola, 2019. OPPOSITE Silkkikuikka (Great-crested Grebe), Maija Isola, 1961, printed using natural indigo for 2021.

beginnings: 'I think that mentality was very evident in the early years of Marimekko, because Finland was in a poor state and people needed functional things for their everyday lives – at the same time, they were ready for an injection of positivity and energy and empowerment.'

Marimekko answered that desire through colour and pattern. Its mission was, and is, born of the marriage of Bauhaus ideals and Finnish culture: to bring hope and joy to everyday life through timeless designs that retain a sense of the hands that made them, even when they are mechanically reproduced. The name Marimekko remains in circulation, and retains its value, because of its ideological foundations. Armi Ratia was a champion of freedom, equality and self-expression, and the company continues to support those beliefs. 'We believe that there cannot be any joy without fairness and equality', says Alahuhta-Kasko today. As the company continues to expand, a sensitivity to and awareness of differences in terms of culture and climate is ever more important, and sure to be aided by technology.

Data did not drive Armi, instinct did. 'Lifestyle', the now-prevalent concept that she pioneered, has become an umbrella term denoting good-looking products for the home. As one of the hundreds of thousands of Finns displaced by the war, Armi understood better than most the importance of home, and the sense of wholeness and security that comes from having a place to call one's own. 'The importance of home as your own sanctuary has not gone anywhere', observes Alahuhta-Kasko in 2020. 'I think that it's even further accentuated, with the pandemic and the overall uncertainty in the world.'

For seventy years, Marimekko has been a constant in a changing world. During that time, it has become an integral part of Finnish heritage. Part

ABOVE Tarhuri (Gardener), Maija Louekari, 2019.
OPPOSITE Marimekko has been collaborating with Spinnova, creators of responsible wood-based textiles that are recyclable, free of harmful chemicals and produced with water conservation in mind, since 2017. The prototype garments seen here are an innovative manifestation of Marimekko's design classics.

OPPOSITE Vuosirenkaat (Tree Rings), Tytti Laitakari, 2020.
ABOVE LEFT The first Marimekko co-created capsule collection, made in collaboration with the graphic designers Antti Kekki and Matts Bjolin, was released in 2021. It blends archival images with Marimekko's iconic prints – here collaged on a t-shirt – to reinterpret the 'essence of Marimekko'.
ABOVE RIGHT Taking the famous Unikko poppy into another new dimension is the unisex Huipennus sweatshirt, which features a padded and embossed flower at centre front.

of the Marimekko magic is that it has universal appeal while managing to remain true to its roots. 'What is the reason that it's so easy to fall in love [with Marimekko]?' muses Sanna-Kaisa Niikko, Marimekko's Chief Marketing Officer. 'Maybe because Marimekko prints are thought of as pieces of art, and art is a universal language. It's easy to understand no matter which culture you come from. That's how Armi Ratia started: she got a group of young creative artists around her and asked them to create beautiful, bold patterns for Marimekko. Many of the patterns are inspired by nature, which is again something that reflects back to the lives of people everywhere.'

Finland, notes Niikko with some pride, has thrice been named the happiest country in the world. Joy is part of the Marimekko DNA, as is authenticity, which, Alahuhta-Kasko notes, people are increasingly drawn to in a digital age, echoing similar observations made by Armi.

Armi remains omnipresent at Marimekko. A portrait of the indomitable Finn hangs at the company headquarters, keeping careful watch over all. What would the founder think of Marimekko in the 2020s? She would be 'proud of the fact that, while we honour the legacy and the roots and the heritage of the company, we also have the courage to look forward and understand the way that we can use technology, for example, as a way forward', suggests Alahuhta-Kasko. 'I like to think that she would be proud of us, of our little community.'

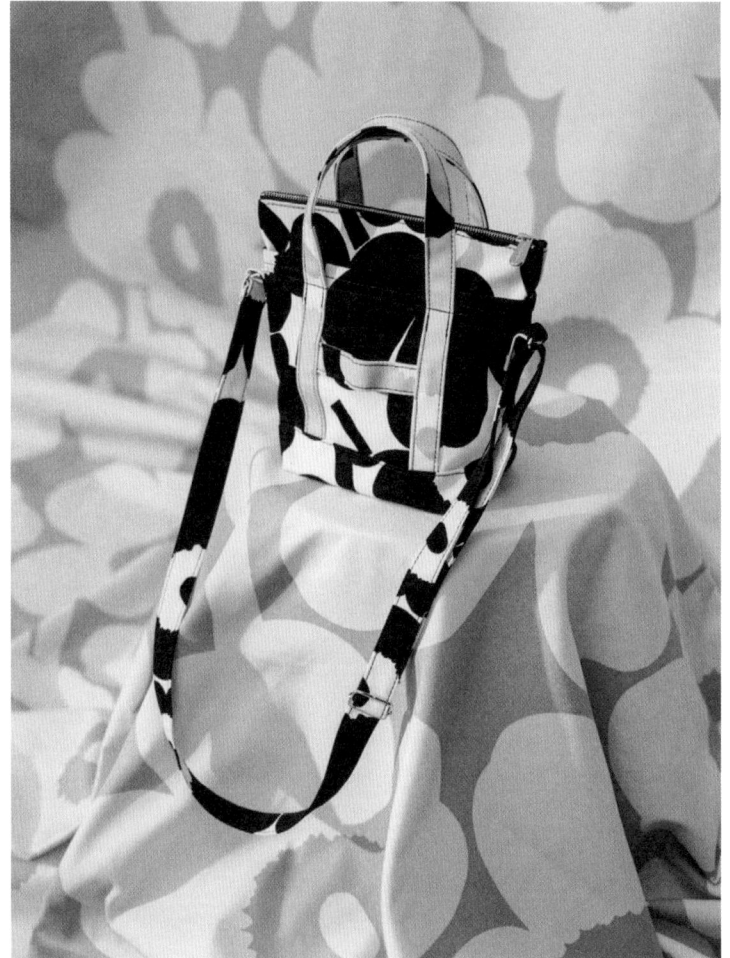

ABOVE Ristomatti Ratia, the founder's son, designed the first Matkuri (Traveller) tote in 1970, and it has been on the go ever since. This version, Milli Matkuri (Milli-Traveller) is patchworked using leftover fabrics printed in two colour-ways of Maija Isola's 1964 Unikko (Poppy) design.
OPPOSITE Marimekko has always focused on timeless garments and motifs – here, the Unikko poppy goes pastel.

Notes

1. Making Marimekko

1 Peggy Polk, 'Woman leads Finnish firm', *Tyler Morning Telegraph*, 10 April 1978, 11
2 Lauren Losson, 'Armi's charm spreads', *Fort Lauerdale News*, 27 September 1972, 27
3 R. W. Apple, "Designer bold enough to sell her fabric", *The Charlotte Observer*, 17 August 1979, 36
4 DISPLAY QUOTE Estelle Bond Guralnick, 'Marimekko on the go', *The Boston Globe*, 5 December 1975, 347
5 Astrid Lindgren, *War Diaries 1939-1945* (New Haven, CT, 2016), transl. Sarah Death, foreword by Karin Nyman, p. 8
6 R. W. Apple, 'Designer Rose From Ashes of WWII', *Intelligencer Journal*, 15 August 1979, 12
7 Hall Piper, 'The shortest distance to success is colorful simplicity', *The Baltimore Sun*, 13 January 1976, 17
8 R. W. Apple, 'Designer Rose From Ashes of WWII', *Intelligencer Journal*, 15 August 1979, 12
9 Estelle Bond Guralnick, 'Marimekko on the go', *The Boston Globe*, 5 December 1975, 347
10 DISPLAY QUOTE Barbara Varro, 'Marimekko stylist no "simple old lady"', *The Morning Call* via *The Chicago Sun Times*, 19 October 1975, 93
11 Dean Pritchard, 'A Matter of Taste', *Chicago Tribune*, 10 April 1967, 46
12 Jo Woestendiek, 'A new bedtime story translated into English', *The News and Observer*, 24 September 1972, 48
13 Diana Loercher, 'Marimekko boasts color', *Green Bay Press Gazette*, 15 October 1972, 24
14 'WHAT WE DO - Vuokko Nurmesniemi', interview for 'ORNAMO 100' exhibition <www.youtube.com/watch?v=amwCg0EzBvU> [accessed October 2020]
15 Barbara Varro, 'Marimekko stylist no "simple old lady"', *The Morning Call* via *The Chicago Sun Times*, 19 October 1975, 93
16 Julia Byrne, 'Designer dynamo. Fabrics: Start to Finnish', *The Los Angeles Times*, 6 March 1968, 59
17 Barbara Varro, 'Marimekko stylist no "simple old lady"', *The Morning Call* via *The Chicago Sun Times*, 19 October 1975, 93
18 Madeleine Morley, 'How Marimekko Became a Majority Women Design Powerhouse', *Eye on Design*, 10 May 2016 <eyeondesign.aiga.org/how-marimekko-became-a-majority-women-design-powerhouse/> [accessed October 2020]
19 Frances Koltun, 'A visit to Helsinki, Finland', *The Journal Times*, 25 March 1962, 32
20 Diana Loercher, 'Marimekko boasts color', *Green Bay Press Gazette*, 15 October 1972, 24
21 Lauren Losson, 'Armi's charm spreads', *Fort Lauerdale News*, 27 September 1972, 27
22 DISPLAY QUOTE Dean Pritchard, 'A Matter of Taste', *Chicago Tribune*, 10 April 1967, 46
23 Beverley Wilson, 'Marimekko', *The Miami Herald*, 13 September 1964, 104
24 Dean Pritchard, 'A Matter of Taste', *Chicago Tribune*, 10 April 1967, 46
25 Lauren Losson, 'Armi's charm spreads', *Fort Lauerdale News*, 27 September 1972, 27
26 DISPLAY QUOTE Quoted in Beverley Wilson, 'Marimekko' *The Miami Herald*, 13 September 1964, 104
27 Frances Koltun, 'A visit to Helsinki, Finland', *The Racine Journal*, 25 March 1962, 32
28 'Her dresses are 'designs', not fashions', *The Windsor Star*, 9 November 1960, 36
29 Anniina Koivu, 'The Aaltos, Modernism with a Human Touch', 18 April 2016 <www.abitare.it/en/research/studies/2016/04/18/alvar-aalto-modernity/> [accessed November 2020]
30 Jane Holtz Kay, 'The Marimekko mystique', *The Boston Globe*, 10 February 1974, 223
31 DISPLAY QUOTE Anne Louise Hitch, 'Winter Cotton, Anyone?', *The Baltimore Sun*, 28 November 1965, 78
32 Jane Holtz Kay, 'The Marimekko mystique', *The Boston Globe*, 10 February 1974, 223
33 Elizabeth Bernkopf, 'Finnish fashions bright and mad', *The Boston Globe*, 14 June 1959, 125
34 Quoted in Laird Borrelli-Persson, 'How the #WFH Movement Could Reshape Fashion', *Vogue.com*, 1 September 2020 <www.vogue.com/article/independent-fashion-designers-on-decentralization-living-and-working-far-from-fashion-capitals> [accessed November 2020]
35 DISPLAY QUOTE Dilys Rowe, 'Shaped by History', *The Observer*, 16 September 1962, 26
36 CAPTION Anne Adams, 'Jackie Kennedy Selects Colorful, Primitive Styles', *The Post-Crescent*, 19 November 1960, 13
37 Miren Arzalluz, 'Balenciaga's Shocking Bodies', *Interwoven: The fabric of things* <kvadratinterwoven.com/balenciagas-shocking-bodies> [accessed October 2020]
38 Dilys Rowe, 'Shaped by History', *The Observer*, 16 September 1962, 26
39 'Gay Fashions from Finland', *LIFE*, 24 June 1966, 71
40 CAPTION 'Nurmesniemi and Rimala – Creating Marimekko Design' <guides.hamhelsinki.fi/en/work/nurmesniemi-and-rimala-creating-marimekko-design> [accessed November 2020]
41 Dean Pritchard, 'A Matter of Taste', *Chicago Tribune*, 10 April 1967, 46
42 Eloise Dungan, 'Putting the Finnish touch on an opening', *The San Francisco Examiner*, 17 October 1973, 26
43 *Ibid.*
44 DISPLAY QUOTE Florence de Santis, 'One Touch of Fashion', *The Shreveport Times*, 22 March 1963, 21
45 DISPLAY QUOTE Eugenia Sheppard, 'Intellectuals go for uniform', *Hartford Courant*, 14 November 1963, 28
46 Jane Holtz Kay, 'The Marimekko mystique', *The Boston Globe*, 10 February 1974, 228
47 Jane Thompson and Alexandra Lange, *Design Research: The Store That Brought Modern Living to American Homes* (New York, NY, 2010)
48 Elizabeth Bernkopf, 'Finnish dresses blend flapper, sack looks', *The Boston Globe*, 1 December 1959, 68
49 Eugenia Sheppard, 'Intellectuals go for uniform', *Hartford Courant*, 14 November 1963, 28
50 'Next First Lady leader in fashion', *Fort Worth Star-Telegram*, 12 November 1960, 11
51 Eugenia Sheppard, 'Danger of extinction also faces fashions', *The Ottawa Citizen*, 6 September 1962, 32
52 Eugenia Sheppard, 'Intellectuals go for uniform', *Hartford Courant*, 14 November 1963, 28
53 Hilary Weaver, 'How a 52-Year-Old Word Invented by a *Vogue* Editor Became 2017's Word of the Year', *Vanity Fair*, 15 December 2017 <www.vanityfair.com/style/2017/12/youthquake-is-oxford-dictionary-word-of-the-year> [accessed October 2020]
54 Maloa Gribkoff, 'Marimekko for bedroom & bath', *The Sacramento Bee*, 23 September 1972, 49
55 Beverley Wilson, 'Marimekko', *The Miami Herald*, 13 September 1964, 104
56 Jane Pierce, 'Flower power is Armi's line', *The Boston Globe*, 22 September 1972, 35
57 R. C. Longworth, 'Armi Ratia is what makes Marimekko tick', *Chicago Tribune*, 19 February 1979, 17
58 DISPLAY QUOTE Dean Pritchard, 'A Matter of Taste', *Chicago Tribune*, 10 April 1967, 46
59 Beverley Wilson, 'Marimekko', *The Miami Herald*, 13 September 1964, 104
60 Rosalie Greenfield, 'Marimekko', *Chicago Tribune*, 19 June 1972, 40
61 'Ratia, Armi', *National Biography of Finland* <kansallisbiografia.fi/english/person/1581> [accessed October 2020]
62 Alison Adburgham, 'Ultima Thule to Soho Square', *The Guardian*, 9 April 1969, 9
63 DISPLAY QUOTE Quoted in Lauren Cochrane, '"A uniform for intellectuals": the fashion legacy of Marimekko', *The Guardian*, 14 March 2018 <www.theguardian.com/fashion/2018/mar/14/uniform-intellectuals-fashion-legacy-marimekko-1950s-colour-postwar-finnish-uniqlo-collaboration> [accessed November 2020]
64 Anne Louise Hitch, 'Winter Cotton, Anyone?', *The Baltimore Sun*, 28 November 1965, 78
65 Sandra Hawk, 'Designer's youth thinking brings patterns with spirit', *Fort Worth Star-Telegram*, 25 September 1972, 17

2. The Art of Printmaking

1 Kay Murphy, 'Trend talk. There's a point to this "stitch in time"', *The Miami Herald*, 4 June 1972, 243
2 Eleanor Lambert, 'Who will design for Lady Bird?', *The Charlotte Observer*, 11 October 1964, 62
3 Maloa Gribkoff, 'Marimekko for bedroom & bath', *The Sacramento Bee*, 23 September 1972, 40
4 Dean Pritchard, 'A Matter of Taste', *Chicago Tribune*, 10 April 1967, 46
5 R. W. Apple, 'Finland's Spirited Designer', *The New York Times*, 2 August 1979, 1
6 *Ibid.*
7 Mary Stanyan, 'Whimsical Styles from Helsinki', *The San Francisco Examiner*, 17 May 1965, 32
8 Jane Pierce, 'Flower power is Armi's line', *The Boston Globe*, 22 September 1972, 35
9 Aleksandra Sorin, 'Marimekko's Unikko Pieni: The Finnish way of experiencing the joy of colours', 23 April 2020 <www.tidsskriftetparagone.com/farger/2020/4/20/marimekkos-unikko-pieni-the-finnish-way-of-experiencing-the-joy-of-colors> [accessed November 2020]
10 Anniina Koivu, 'The Colours of Alvar Aalto', *littala Journal* <www.iittala.com/journal-colours-of-aalto> [accessed November 2020]
11 Dean Pritchard, 'A Matter of Taste', *Chicago Tribune*, 10 April 1967, 46
12 Elizabeth Bernkopf, 'Finnish Fashions Bright and Mad', *The Boston Globe*, 12 June 1959
13 Jane Pierce, 'Flower power is Armi's line', *The Boston Globe*, 22 September 1972, 35
14 *Ibid.*
15 Ralston O'Neill, 'Q&A with Marimekko designer Erja Hirvi', *Dwell* <https://www.dwell.com/collection/qanda-with-marimekko-designer-erja-hirvi-6ba3247e> [accessed October 2020]

3. The Language of Pattern

1 Rosalie Greenfield, 'Marimekko', *Chicago Tribune*, 19 June 1972, 40

Picture List

2 DISPLAY QUOTE Millicent Bowman, 'Speaking in Colors', *Tampa Bay Times*, 10 November 1974, 207

3 'The Finnish fashion', *The Sydney Morning Herald*, 27 October 1960, 30

4 DISPLAY QUOTE Quoted in Lauren Cochrane, '"A uniform for intellectuals": the fashion legacy of Marimekko', *The Guardian*, 14 March 2018 <https://www.theguardian.com/fashion/2018/mar/14/uniform-intellectuals-fashion-legacy-marimekko-1950s-colour-postwar-finnish-uniqlo-collaboration>

5 Maloa Gribkoff, 'Marimekko for bedroom & bath', *The Sacramento Bee*, 23 September 1972, 49

6 'Her dresses are "designs", not fashions', *The Windsor Star*, 9 November 1960, 36

7 Quoted in Hannah Booth, 'Flower Power', *The Guardian*, 5 September 2005 <https://www.theguardian.com/lifeandstyle/2005/sep/05/shopping.fashion> [accessed November 2020]

8 Marilee DesLauriers, 'Marimekko' <fashion-history.lovetoknow.com/fashion-clothing-industry/fashion-designers/marimekko>

9 'Jokapoika by Marimekko' <www.placewares.com/collections/the-every-boy-shirt-jokapoika-by-marimekko> [accessed November 2020]

10 Marimekko advertisement, *The San Francisco Examiner*, 15 May 1984, 16

11 'Armi Ratia, Marimekko Founder and Innovator in Printed Fabrics', *The New York Times*, 4 October 1979 <nyti.ms/1kO6PDH> [accessed November 2020]

12 'Benjamin C. Thompson, Architect of Festive Urban Marketplaces, is Dead', The New York Times, 20 August 2002 <https://www.nytimes.com/2002/08/20/arts/benjamin-c-thompson-84-architect-of-festive-urban-marketplaces-is-dead.html> [accessed November 2020]

13 A. P. Newsfeatures, 'Finnish styles to invade White House', *Lansing State Journal*, 27 November 1960, 62

14 Jo Woestendiek, 'A new bedtime story translated into English', *The Raleigh News and Observer*, 24 September 1972, 48

15 Estelle Bond Guralnick, 'Marimekko on the go', *The Boston Globe*, 5 December 1975, 347

4. Marimekko Next

1 'From birch to dress – new steps in the collaborative Ioncell™ project' <www.marimekko.com/world-of-marimekko/latest-news/collaborative-ioncell-project> [accessed December 2020]

2 Tony Vaccaro/Getty Images

4–5 Pieni Unikko II, Maija Isola, 1964/K. I., 2009

6–7 Osma Harvilahti, September 2020. Model: Melanie Bangura. Outfit: Designmuseum, Helsinki

8–9 Tony Vaccaro/Tony Vaccaro Studio

11 Ismo Kajander/Designmuseum, Helsinki

12 Interfoto/Alamy Stock Photo

13 Helsinki-Helsingfors, Per-Olof Nyström, 1951

14 Tony Vaccaro/Tony Vaccaro Studio

16 Amfora, Maija Isola, 1949

17 Kolmio/Designmuseum, Helsinki

19 Designmuseum, Helsinki

20 Osma Harvilahti, September 2020. Model: Melanie Bangura. Outfit: Designmuseum, Helsinki

23 Seppo Saves/Designmuseum, Helsinki

24 Fotograferna Stig Forsberg & Carl Johan Rönn

26 David Luraschi, Spring/Summer 2020. Models: Elsa Sjökvist, Chawntell Kulkarni

27 Tony Vaccaro/Tony Vaccaro Studio

28 Emma Sarpaniemi, Spring/Summer 2021. Models: Pia Höglund, Sarah Runge, Gunilla Prindal

29 Osma Harvilahti, September 2020. Model: Melanie Bangura

30 Illustrated London News Ltd/Mary Evans

31 Tony Vaccaro/Tony Vaccaro Studio

32 Maurice Miller

33 David Drew Zingg. Photo by SI Cover/*Sports Illustrated* via Getty Images/Getty Images

35 Juhannus colour swatches, Maija Isola, 1966

36 Musta Tamma, Maija Isola, 1954

37 Kaunis Kauris, Teresa Moorhouse, 2011

38 Bryan Saragosa, Summer 2021

39 Bryan Saragosa, Spring 2021

40–41 Janita Autio, May 2019

42 Sebastian Johansson, pre-Spring 2020. Model: Naomi Janumala

43 Osma Harvilahti, limited-edition capsule collection for summer 2019. Model: Aasmae

45 Osma Harvilahti, pre-Spring 2021. Models: Melanie Bangura, Simona Porta

46–47 Tony Vaccaro/Tony Vaccaro Studio

48 Arto Hallakorpi/Designmuseum, Helsinki

51 Osma Harvilahti, September 2020

52 Osma Harvilahti, pre-Fall 2020. Model: Warsan

54 Unikko, Maija Isola, 1964

55 Sebastian Johansson, Spring/Summer 2020. Model: Magda Wolde Selassie

56 Unikko, Maija Isola, 1964

57 Pieni Unikko, Maija Isola, 1964 / K. I., 2009

58 left Pertti Jenytin/Shutterstock

58 centre Unikko colour swatches, Maija Isola, 1964

59 Sebastian Johansson, pre-Spring 2021. Model: Janica Tuominen

61 Osma Harvilahti, September 2020

62–63 Osma Harvilahti, September 2020

64–65 Osma Harvilahti, September 2020

66–67 Oskari Pulkkinen, 2019

68 left Suur Unikko, Maija Isola, 1964 / E.I., 2020

68 right 50th Anniversary Unikko, Maija Isola, 1964 / K.I., 2013

69 Ruutu-Unikko, Maija Isola, 1964 / E.I., 2014

70 Unikko variation, Maija Isola, 1964 / E.I., 2020

71 Workshop, Unikko variation

72 Sebastian Johansson, pre-Spring 2020. Model: Naomi Janumala

72 Osma Harvilahti, Continuous collection, 2020. Model: Utu Armas Karjula

73 Juho Huttunen, Winter 2020

74, 75 Hennika, Vuokko Eskolin-Nurmesniemi, 1953

76 Indus, Vuokko Eskolin-Nurmesniemi, 1953

77 Husaari, Maija Isola, 1966

78 Suolampi, Vuokko Eskolin-Nurmesniemi, 1959

79 Nadja, Vuokko Eskolin-Nurmesniemi, 1959

80, 81 Mansikkavuoret, Maija Isola, 1969

82 Ostjakki, Fujiwo Ishimoto, 1983

83 Jäkälä, Fujiwo Ishimoto, 1983

84, 85 Kumiseva, Katsuji Wakisaka, 1971

86 Kivet colour swatches, Maija Isola, 1956

87 Isot Kivet, Maija Isola, 1959

88, 89 Maalaisruusu, Maija Isola, 1964

90, 91 Silkkikuikka, Maija Isola, 1961

92 Raide, Annika Rimala, 1966

93 Nauru, Fujiwo Ishimoto, 1981

94, 95 Rötti, Vuokko Eskolin-Nurmesniemi, 1953

96, 97 Ukkospilvi, Fujiwo Ishimoto, 1981

98, 99 Putkinotko, Maija Isola, 1957

100 Erja Hirvi, Lumimarja sketches

101–3 Lumimarja, Erja Hirvi, 2004

104 top left Bryan Saragosa, Spring 2021

104 top right Erja Hirvi, Ruudut paper-cut sketch

104 bottom right Oiva/Ruudut mug

105 Ruudut, Erja Hirvi, Maija Louekari, Aino-Maija Metsola, Jenni Tuominen, 2019

106 Teija Puranen, Teippi contact-paper sketch

107 Teippi, Teija Puranen, 2013

108 Koski, Fujiwo Ishimoto, 1986

109 Vattenblänk, Astrid Sylwan, 2010

110–111 Claire Aho. © Jussi Brofeldt

112 Timo Kirves

115 Karuselli, Katsuji Wakisaka, 1973

116 Unikko, Maija Isola, 1964

117 Kerttu Malinen, 2015

118 Joonas, Maija Isola, 1961

119 above Arto Hallakorpi/Designmuseum, Helsinki

119 below Pietinen/Designmuseum, Helsinki

120 Designmuseum, Helsinki

121 Pikku Suomu, Annika Rimala, 1965

122 Chris Vidal Tenomaa, Summer 2016. Model: Saara Sihvonen

123 Kivet, Maija Isola, 1956

124 Siirtolapuutarha, Maija Louekari, 2009

125 Lokki, Maija Isola, 1961

126 Sebastian Nurmi

127 Oona, Maija Isola, 1968

128, 129 Muija, Maija Isola, 1968

130 Liito, Maija Isola, 1983

131 Nasti, Vuokko Eskolin-Nurmesniemi, 1957

132 Varvunraita, Vuokko Eskolin-Nurmesniemi, 1958

133 Pirput Parput, Vuokko Eskolin-Nurmesniemi, 1957

134 Kuiskaus, Fujiwo Ishimoto, 1981

135 Tuubiraita, Jenni Tuominen, 2017

136 Siluetti, Carina Seth Andersson, 2016

137 Taivas, Fujiwo Ishimoto, 1985

138 Matti Saanio/Finnish Museum of Photography, Helsinki

139 Designmuseum, Helsinki

140–41 Tony Vaccaro/Tony Vaccaro Studio

142 Osma Harvilahti, September 2020. Model: Melanie Bangura. Outfit: Designmuseum, Helsinki

143 Bruno Werzinski, Spring/Summer 2017. Model: Thea Arvidsson

144 Osma Harvilahti, September 2020. Model: Melanie Bangura. Outfit: Designmuseum, Helsinki

145 Tony Vaccaro/Tony Vaccaro Studio

146 Osma Harvilahti, September 2020. Model: Melanie Bangura

147 Tony Vaccaro/Tony Vaccaro Studio

148 Bengt Erwald, *Svenska Damtidning*, May 1966/Designmuseum, Helsinki

149 Emma Sarpaniemi, Spring/Summer 2021. Model: Gunilla Prindal

150 Kuuma, Fujiwo Ishimoto, 1978

151 Vikuri, Erja Hirvi, 2018

152 Primavera, Maija Isola, 1972

153 Kasvio, Lotta Maija, 2018

154 Puketti, Annika Rimala, 1965

155 Kukkaketo, Fujiwo Ishimoto, 1975

156 Kukkatori, Maija Isola, 1970

157 Mehiläinen, Maija Isola, 1973

158 Juhannustaika, Aino-Maija Metsola, 2007

159 Viivakukka, Satu Maaranen, 2016

160 Designmuseum, Helsinki

161 Osma Harvilahti, September 2020. Model: Melanie Bangura. Outfit: Designmuseum, Helsinki

162, 163 Keidas, Annika Rimala, 1967

164 Jokeri, Annika Rimala, 1967

165 Osma Harvilahti, September 2020. Model: Melanie Bangura. Outfit: Designmuseum, Helsinki

166 Designmuseum, Helsinki

167 Iso Laine, Annika Rimala, 1965

168 Seireeni, Maija Isola, 1964

169 Petrooli, Annika Rimala, 1963

170 left Melooni, Maija Isola, 1963

170 right Osma Harvilahti, limited-edition capsule collection for summer 2019. Model: Aasmae

Acknowledgments

With thanks to everyone at Marimekko and Thames & Hudson who has worked so hard to bring this book together, to the author, Laird Borrelli-Persson, and to the photographers, models, designers, museums and archives listed on p. 269, who kindly provided many of the images on these pages.

Index

Illustrations are in **bold**.

A tote bag to celebrate Marimekko's seventieth anniversary.